To Dorothea, Scarlet, Loris and Elvera

ONOMATOPOEIA
THE PORT
Charles Avery

Le Plateau / Frac Île-de-France, Paris
Kunstverein Hannover
Ex3 Centro per l'arte contemporanea, Firenze
Koenig Books, London

PROLOGUE

I first came to the Island at the end of the great kelp rush, although I was not aware of that at the time. On the contrary I had sought this land with a view to being its discoverer.

When I dragged my boat onto the remote shore it was with the last of my strength, for I had fought the tide and the rain and the forests of seaweed that wrapped around my oars.

I threw down my bag, leant my gun against a large rock, and peeled a banana.

I could not see far for it was dark and large raindrops inundated my eyes, so I listened. I heard the bladderack crackling in the sway, the patter of the rain on the clay, and the cracks and hoots of unknown beasts going about their close lives.

As I tucked into a second banana I started to fantasize about the reception that would await me on my return to Triangland: the flag-wavers on the pier, an interview with *Fancy That* magazine, a message from the government.

As I savoured that feeling of utter fulfillment, I became aware, out of the corner of my eye, of something stirring. Turning my head I saw - trying to camouflage itself amongst a cluster or rocks — a Stone-mouse: part animal, part mineral, whose heart beats only once every thousand years, and for whom even the slightest movement is an agonizing contortion. I would bring this novel being home and present it to the Premier as a souvenir of this remarkable new world. So I took an old pickle jar from my bag and started to scoop the creature in together with some of its damp environment. The rain had begun to fall heavily now and horrible little noises were emanating from the darkness, the source of which seemed to be getting closer. I tried to ignore them.

As I screwed the lid tight however, I was startled by another more familiar sound: that of Humanity.

As I turned towards the land I could make out a pale figure coming towards me across the shore: a young woman it emerged, carrying a basket, hopping from rock to rock, talking, apparently to herself. She was dressed in a chemise, soaked and muddied around the hem, a light cardigan, and rubber boots. She appeared to be smitten by some kind of weed that she intermittently stopped to harvest from the rocks, completely oblivious to my presence.

I took my gun off my shoulder and raised it, a gesture she ignored, leading me to suspect she was no more than a ghost. Just as it seemed she would pass right through me, she looked up and spoke. "The Grass is Alive."

Her face, it dawned on me, was beautiful.

I composed myself and replied "Naturally it is alive."

"nO", she said. "The GraSs is AliVe."

I saw what she was driving at, for this strange weed seemed to squirm, yet didn't move. Rather, it continued to reoccupy the same space, twisting like a corkscrew on its own perverse axis.

"This isn't real." I asserted, alluding to the general situation.

"Everything is real", she replied succinctly.

At that moment, out of the darkness, sprang the causes of the horrible little noises – I let off a trembling shot. Three slavering beasts attended her side.

"Don't shoot", she said calmly, as if I hadn't a hope of hitting anything. "They're mine. Don't be afraid".

Imagine the contrast of emotions I experienced on the shore that day. I had landed there believing myself an explorer of the first order, namer of a new realm and all things in it, only to find out I had been beaten to it by this slight, inadequately dressed girl who was apparently prospering. Simultaneously I had fallen in love.

Through a series of misunderstandings I came to believe that her name was Miss Miss and she that I was called Only McFew. Miss Miss was to become my companion and sponsor on the Island – while consistently and skillfully eschewing my further overtures.

That night I slept under my coat on an old chaise longue in the corridor of her apartment, in the town of Onomatopoeia – for it transpired that I was not even the first man to set foot here but that I had been preceded by several generations of pilgrims, prospectors, rushers, law-makers and law-breakers, entrepreneurs, itinerants, missionaries, mystics and skalds, who had all come through this port.

I was awoken early by the rancid breath of one of her pets upon my face. Stiff and disorientated, I arose slowly so as not to alarm the creature and provoke an unpredictable reaction, and padded across the corridor into the main room.

It was simple and vivid in design. The floor was tiled in alternate black, grey and white hexagons and the walls were painted brilliant pink. There was a table with some of the precious grass in a vase and a large window. On the far side of the room was another exhibit that attracted me. Placed on a white cuboid by the wall was what appeared to be a tank, inside of which four winged things fluttered around one another. There was a strange symmetry to their dance and as I came closer I saw that occasionally they passed without the structure that at first appeared to contain them. I reached my hand out to touch the glass, but there was none.

"They don't stay there because they have to, they stay because they like it," explained Miss Miss who had appeared immaculately in the room. "Tea?"

After a frugal breakfast Miss Miss told me to leave and come back later as she had an impresario coming to see her animals, which apparently she had been teaching to sing. She suggested I take a walk around the town, and gave me some currency with which to buy lunch. Afterwards, she said, we should go back to the shore where I left my boat, as the kelp-rushers may find it and destroy it if they thought it belonged to a competitor.

As I walked anonymously through the port I was bewildered by the energy and variety of the place and wondered at my naivety for having believed myself to be the first person to set foot on these shores.

Hundreds of tourists came streaming down the gangplanks of great passenger liners that buffeted the pier, who would be inundated by a throng of peddlers, pushers, prostitutes and guides, as soon as they disembarked.

There were cafés, fast food cabins, ladies with shopping bags from expensive boutiques... a gaggle of schoolgirls on tour said something lewd to me and then broke into peels of laughter as they moved on.

Further along the shore there were signs of industry, and recession: warehouses, great defunct turbines, a large shelter with a sign on the roof saying LABOUR. Inside were some long benches, a couple of derelict fruit machines, an urn and a man sitting at a table wearing a black peaked cap with a red circle on the front – sorting tickets.

Just outside a group of itinerants were involved in some alternative economy.

I amounted to no more than they did now, yet somehow I felt liberated by my bankruptcy: I was a nobody with nothing to prove, free to explore this other country which was no longer my responsibility but simply something new to be perceived.

It was also an opportunity to contemplate my future, for I did not much fancy an ignominious return home, and here on the Island there was the attraction of Miss Miss, not that she seemed moved by me, and I assessed that she was more likely to evict me from her corridor than allow me into her bedroom.

I exercised my new status as tourist by standing in line to purchase a poke of moules and two eggs from *Marcel's Casserole*.

My thinking was that I needed to impress her, so she would look at me in a different light from that of the bedraggled, deluded stray she rescued from the shore.

Still I reckoned she must have noticed something that distinguished me from the multitude of other destitutes who had come here, in order for her to invite me so insouciantly into her home. Was it my soft complexion? Other-worldliness? Wine-coloured gumboots with black soles? Natural aristocracy?

The egg was so disgustingly bitter it made me wince, but I persevered with it.

An old woman brushed past in a spiky black hat, which almost took my eye out. It looked like a giant urchin on her head. She walked quickly and seemed cross. On her heels, reasoning with her, was a man in a suit who addressed her as 'mother'.

Amongst the crowds, standing in front of the Penrose Trading Company, I spotted a pair of gentlemen who interested me, who seemed to be about something different than the hordes of day-trippers, so I hovered behind them.

They were heavily dressed in thick jumpers, big coats and fine leather boots, and they had a trolley packed with equipment: guns, cages, and large amounts of pristine rope, water cans, and more leather boots.

I couldn't hear their conversation, but they were conferring over a map, not an ordinary street plan with sites of interest denoted but a great unfolded sheet - which they had trouble managing in the wind - covered in arcane contours and points and symbols.

I bit into my second egg.

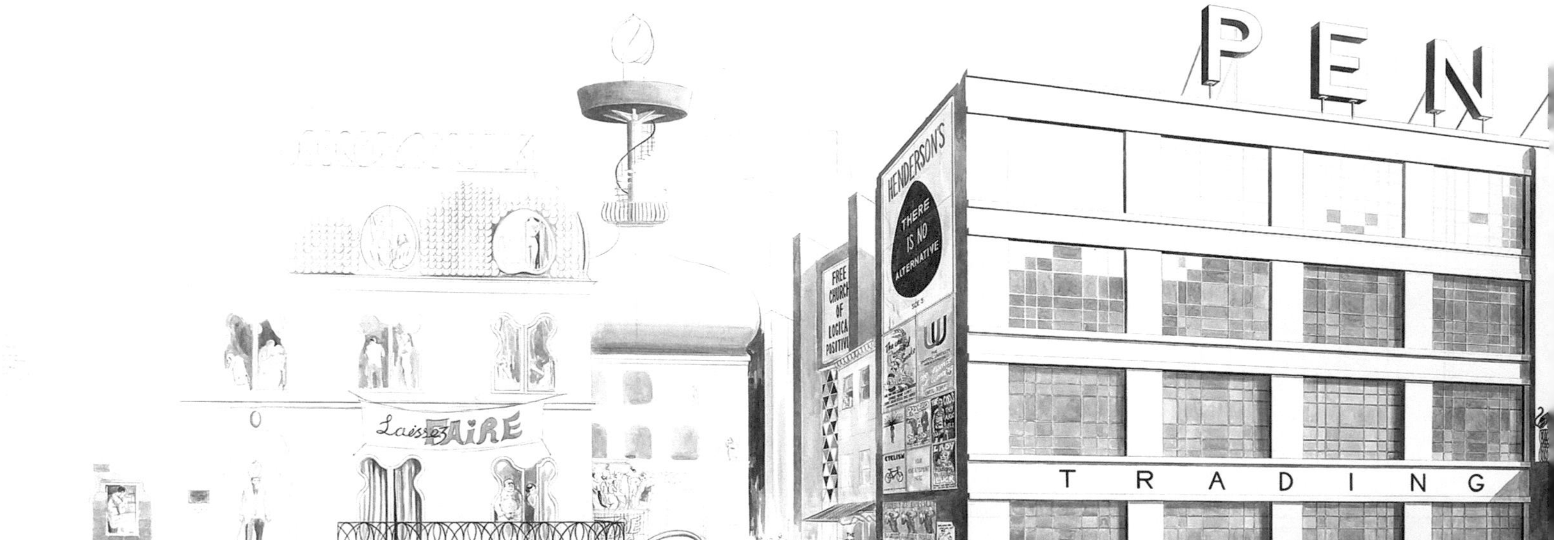

PEN
HENDERSON'S
THERE IS NO ALTERNATIVE
Laissez FAIRE
TRADING
HEAVY
RIANGLANDERS TENDE
PROPER STAT!

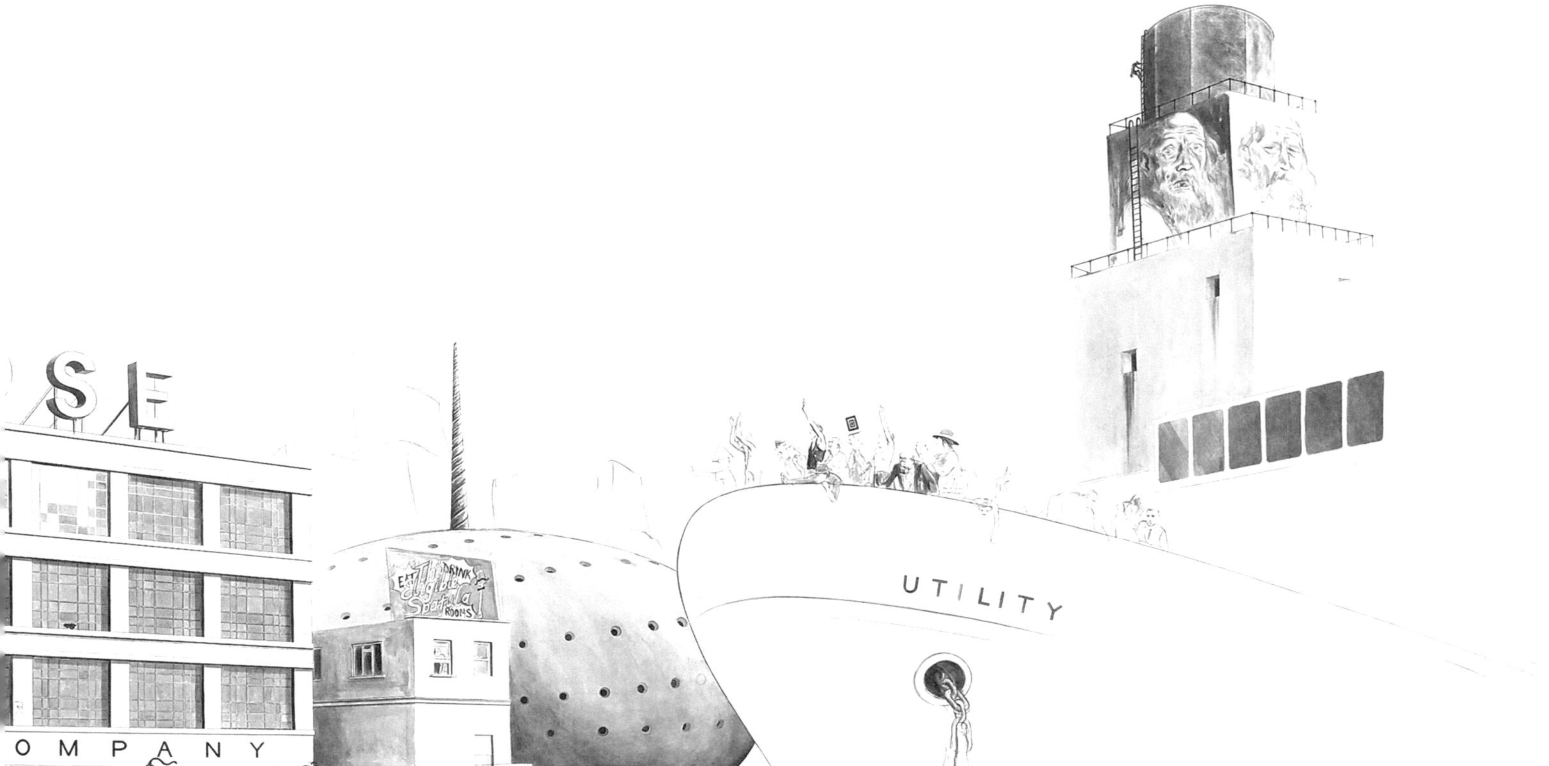
SE
OMPANY
IDENTITY
DUTY
UTILITY

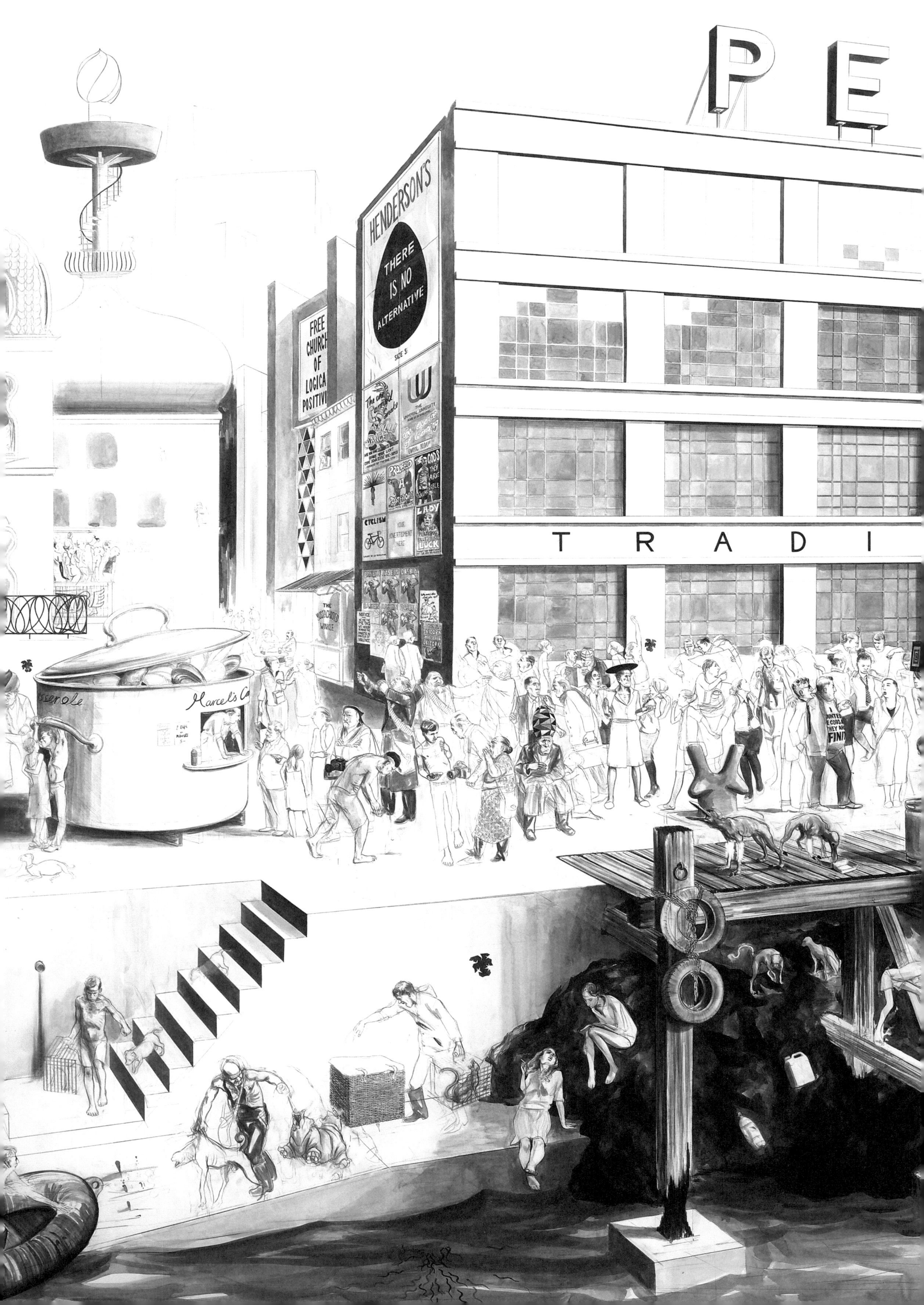

PE
HENDERSON'S
THERE IS NO ALTERNATIVE
SIZE 5
FREE CHURCH OF LOGICA POSITIVI
The one armed Snake
SKILL! CHANCE
THE UNIVERSAL UNIVERSITY
the essence of learning
ENROL TODAY
THE GODS THEY ARE
CYCLISM
YOUR ADVERTISMENT HERE
LADY AND HER PLATYPUS
LUCK
DASEIN
NOTICE
UNICORN
THE MUSTACHIOED WINKLE
Marcel's
TRADI

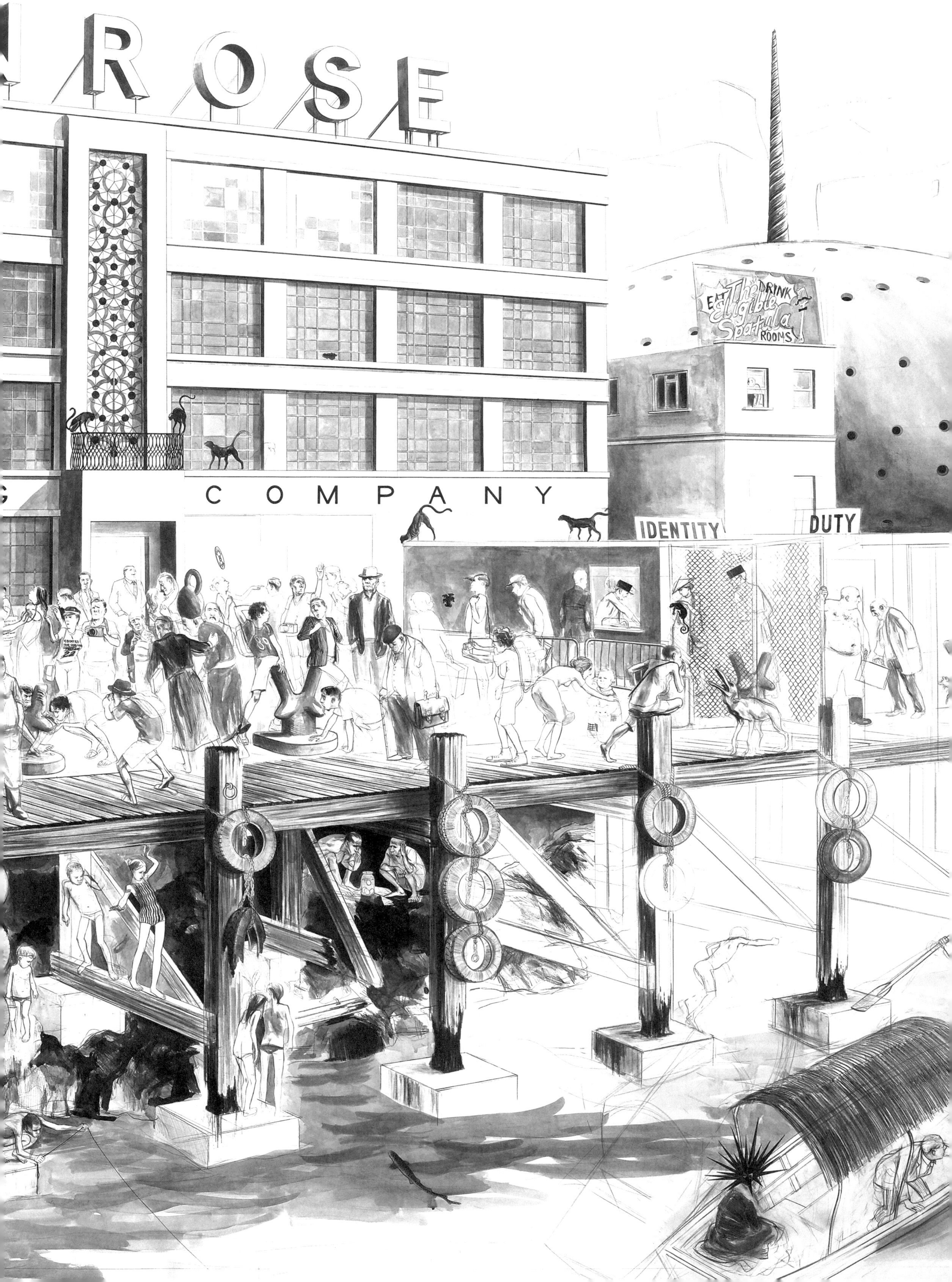

ROSE
EAT The DRINK
Eligible Spatula
ROOMS
COMPANY
IDENTITY
DUTY

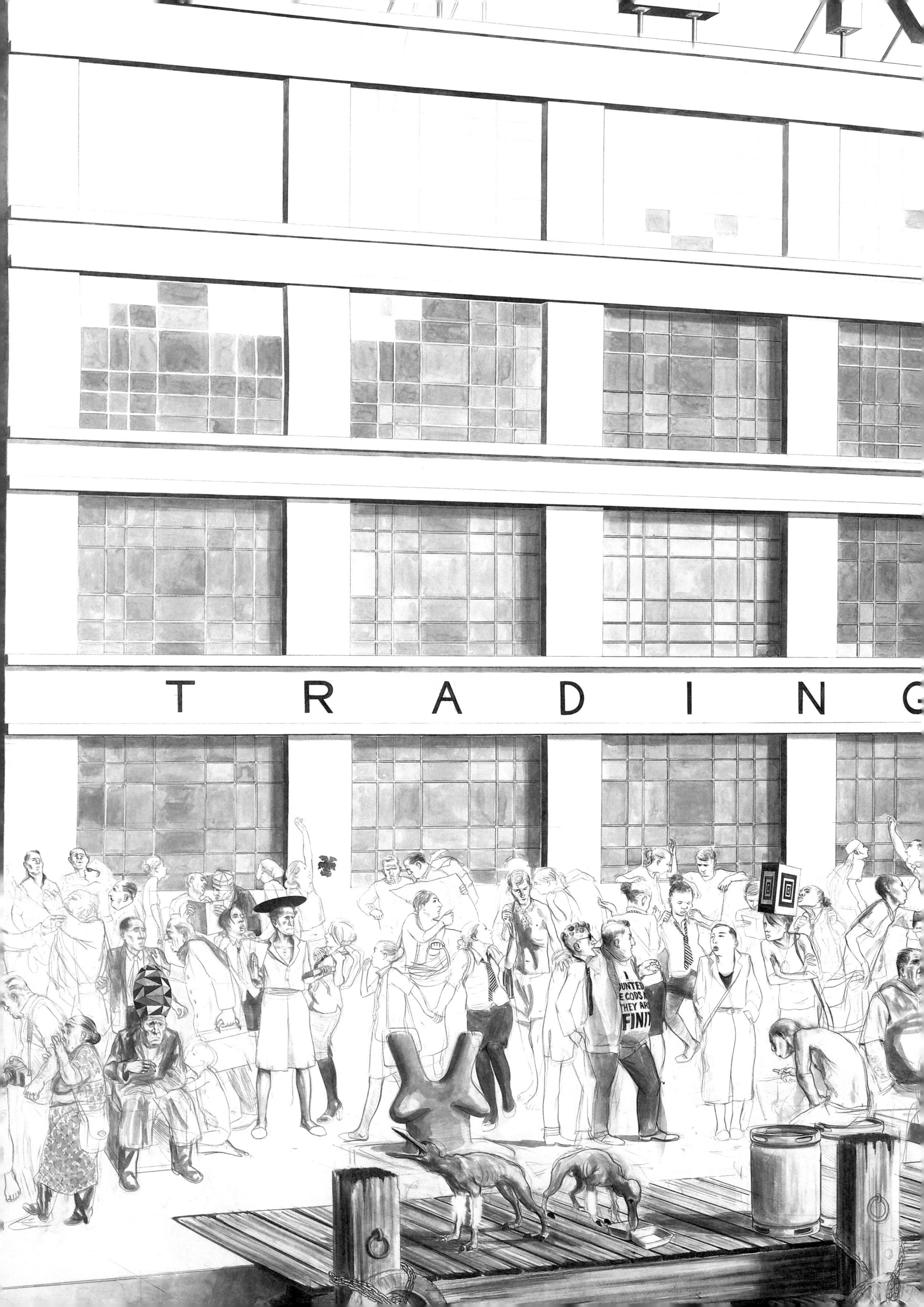

TRADING
I
UNTED
E GODS A
THEY AR
FINIT

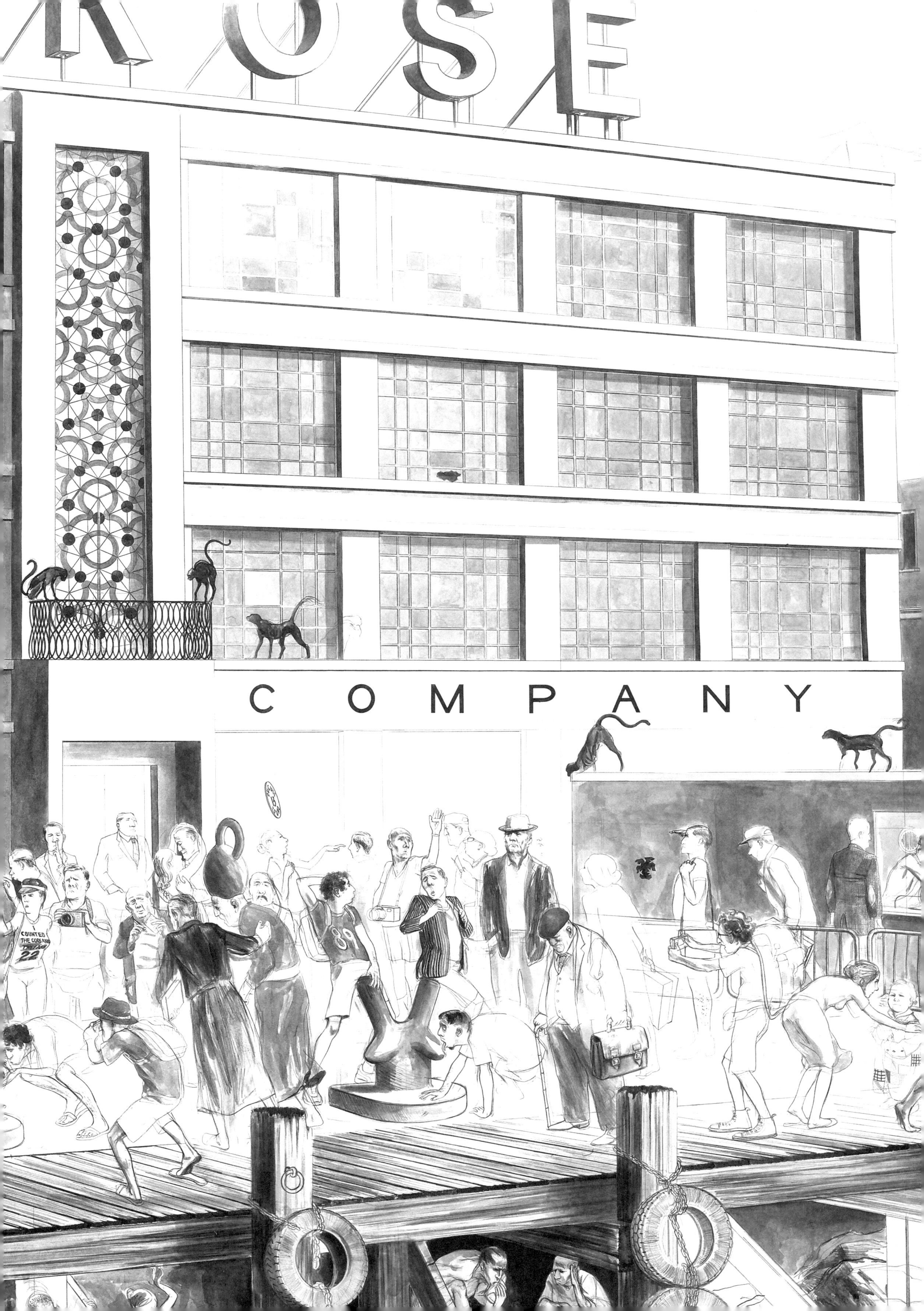
COMPANY

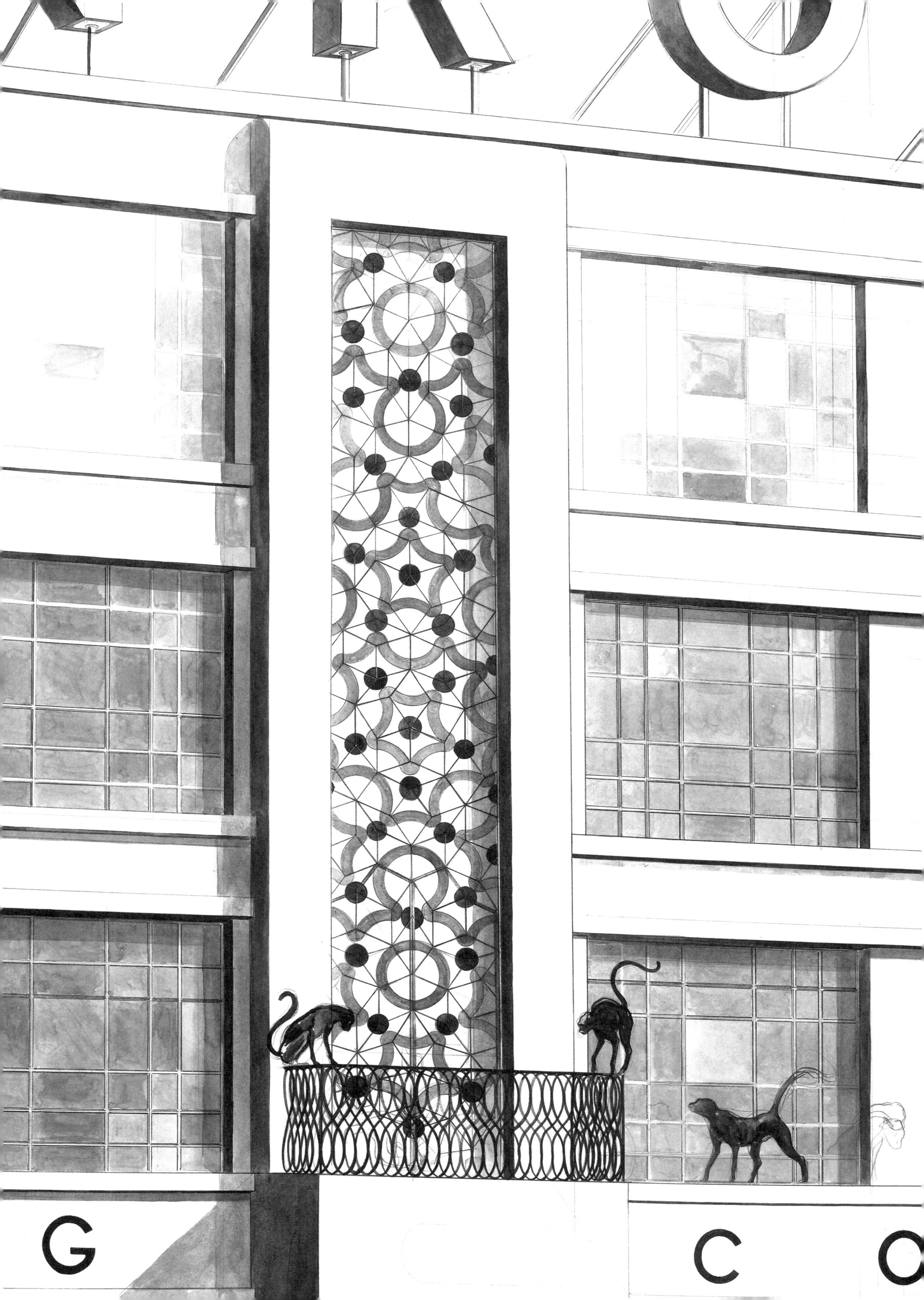
G
C

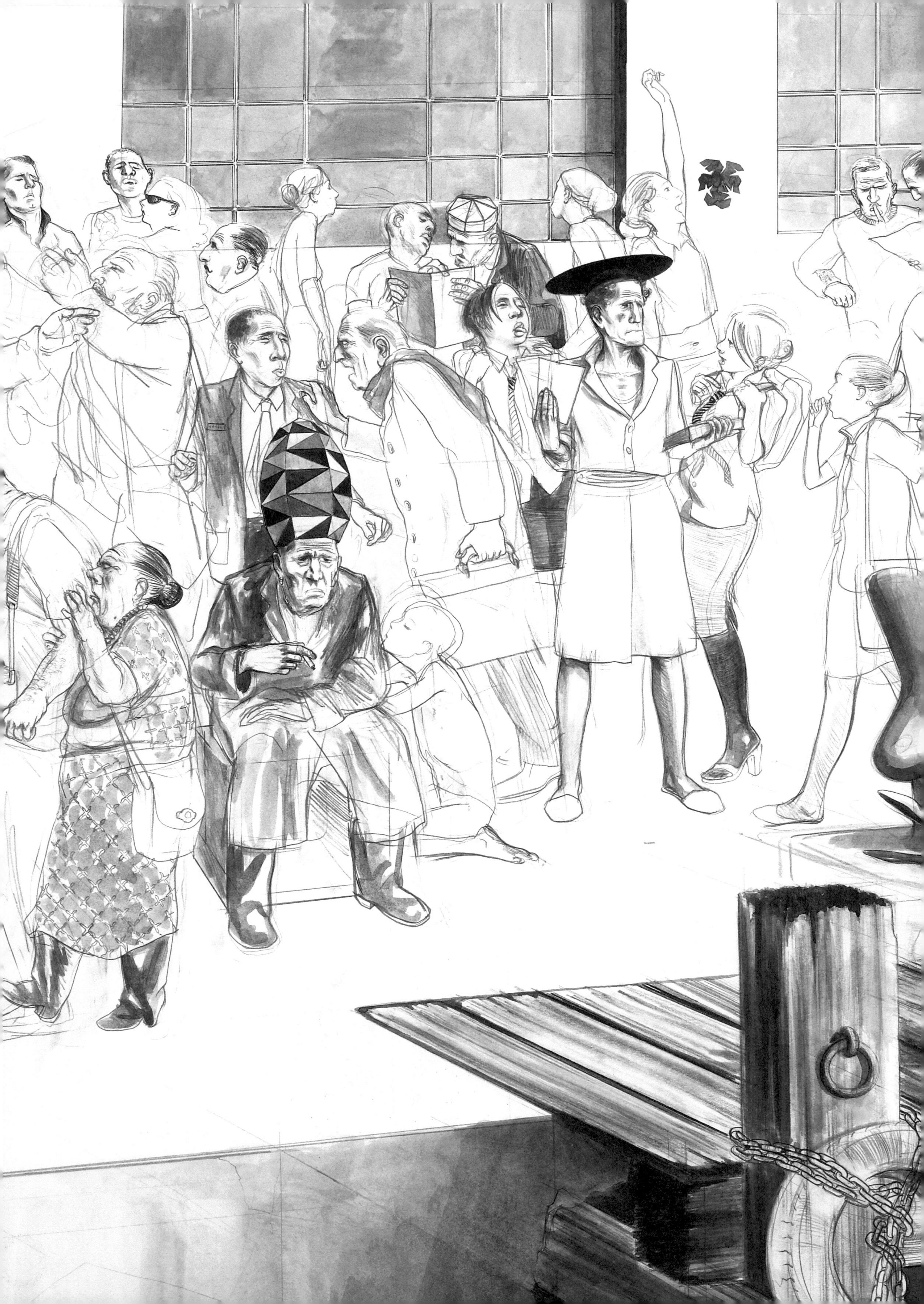

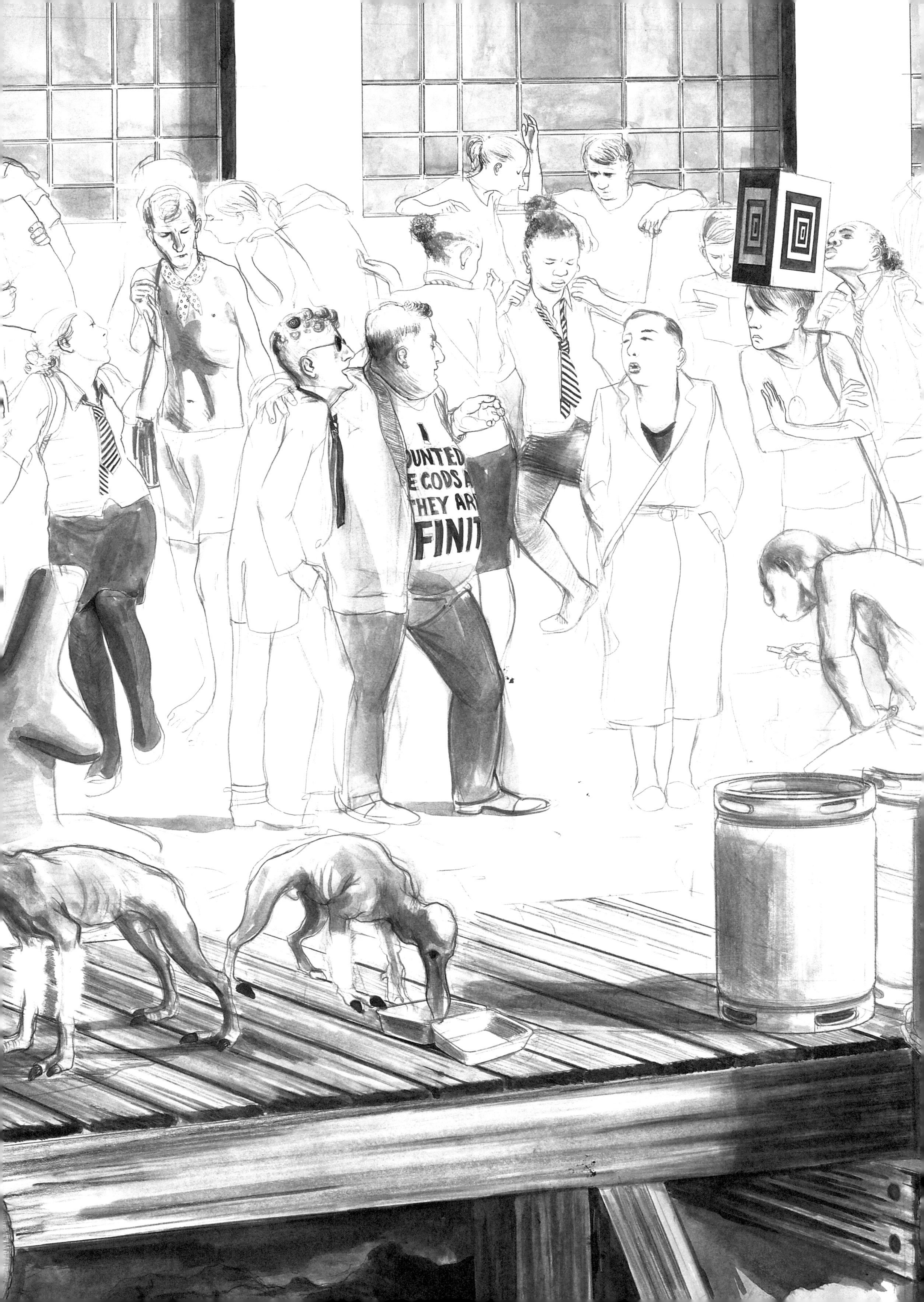
I
UNTED
E CODS A
THEY AR
FINIT

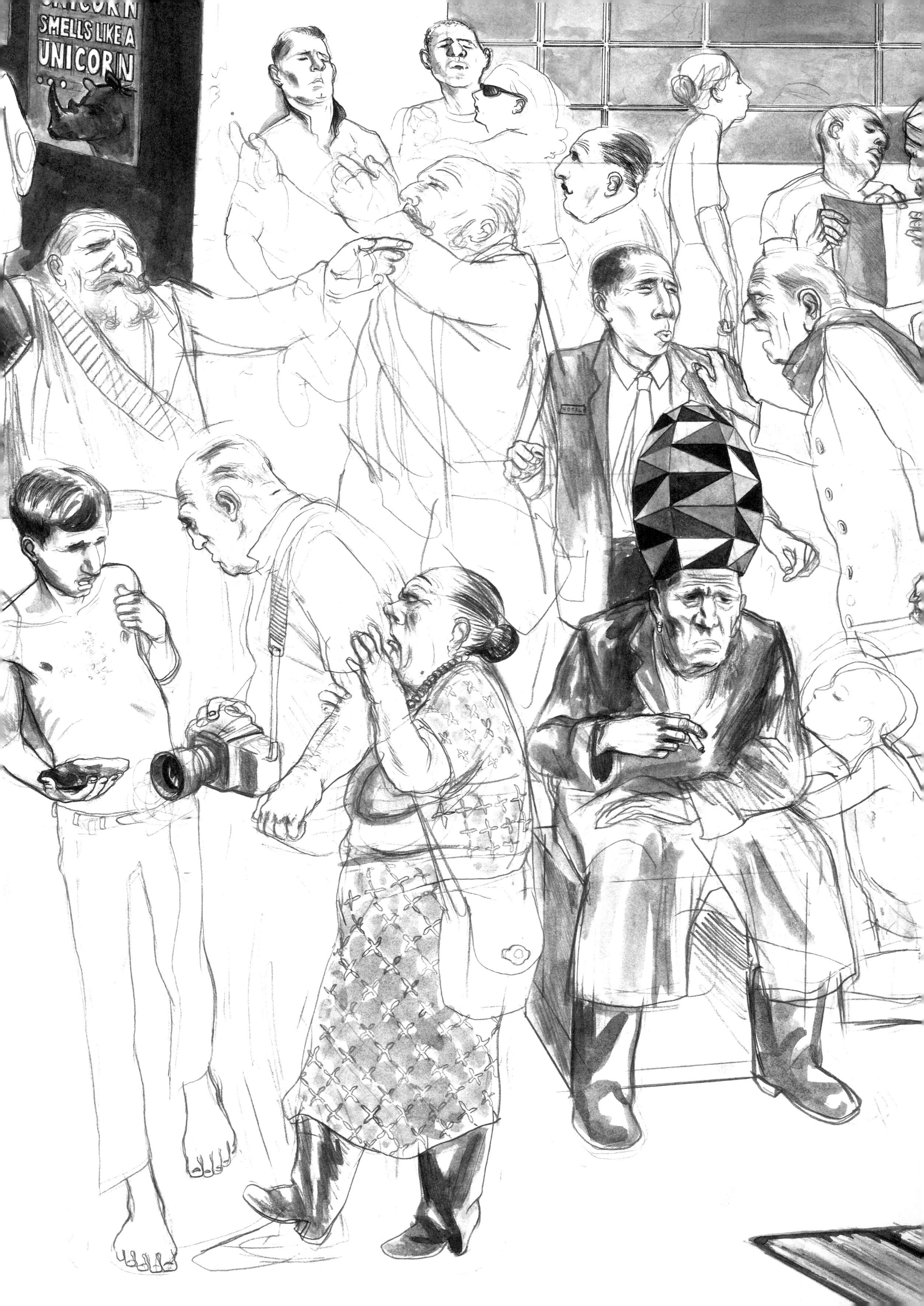
SMELLS LIKE A
UNICORN

O M P A

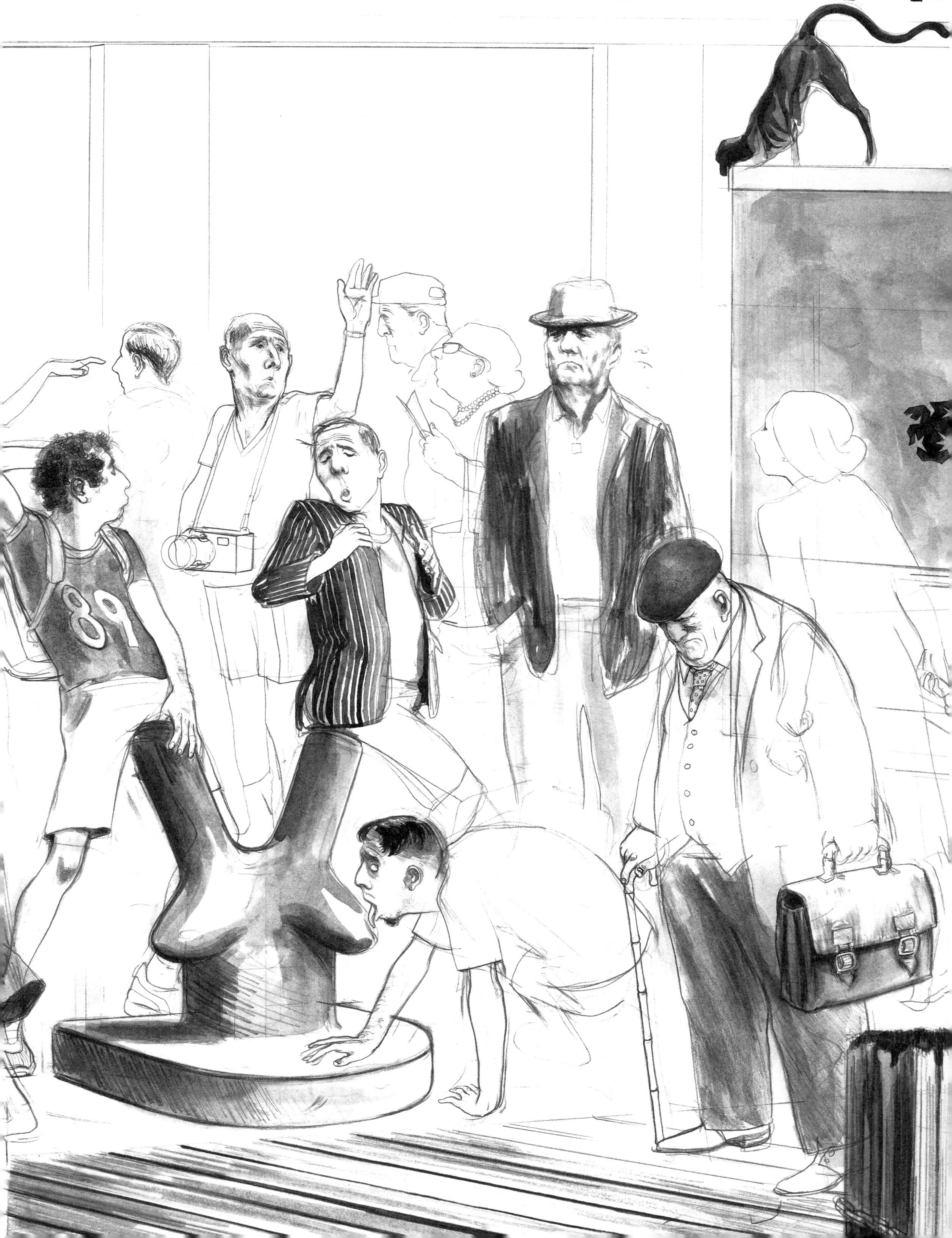

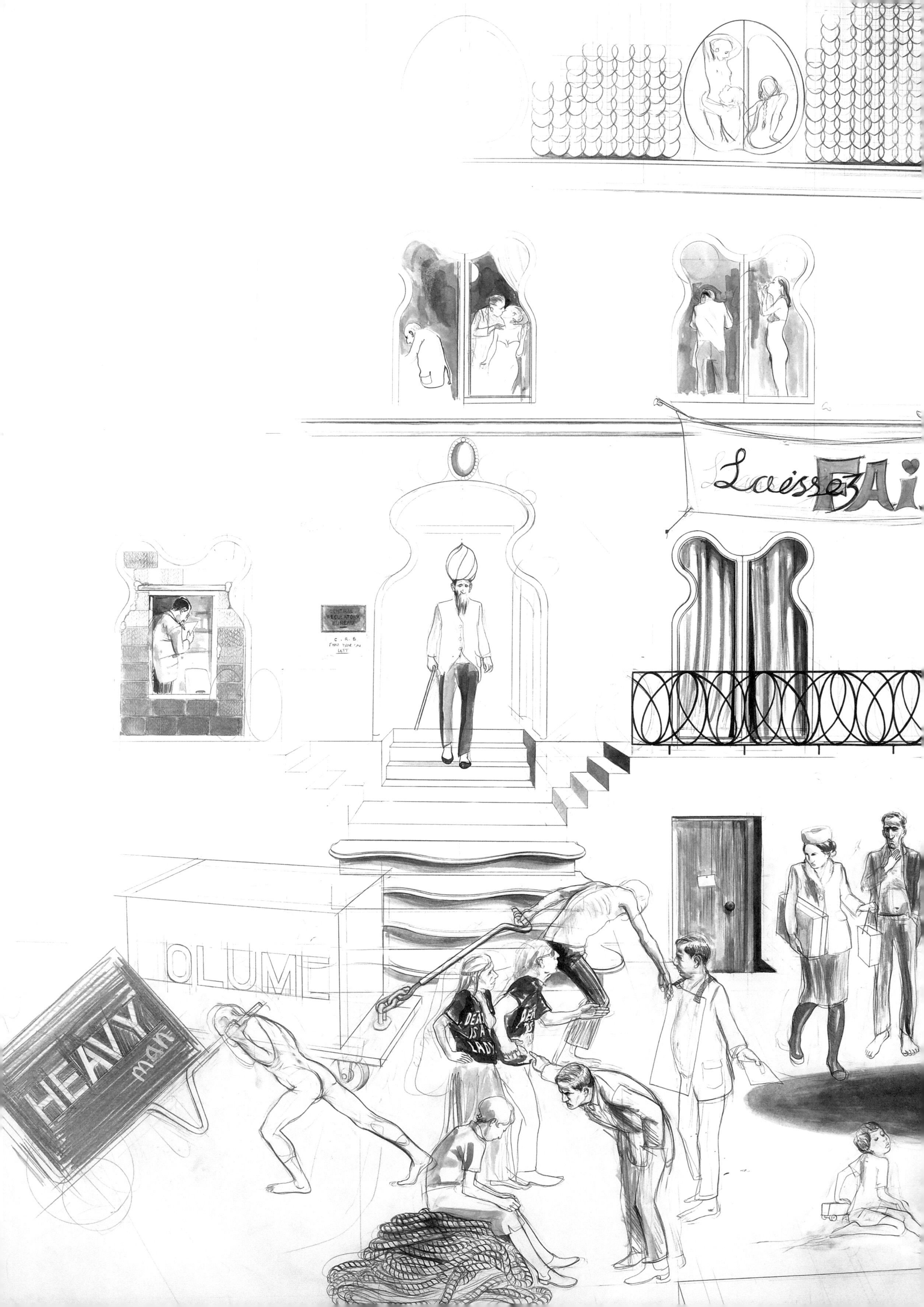
Laissez FAi
CENTRAL REGULATORY BUREAU
C.R.B
FIRST DOOR ON LEFT
OLUME
HEAVY
man

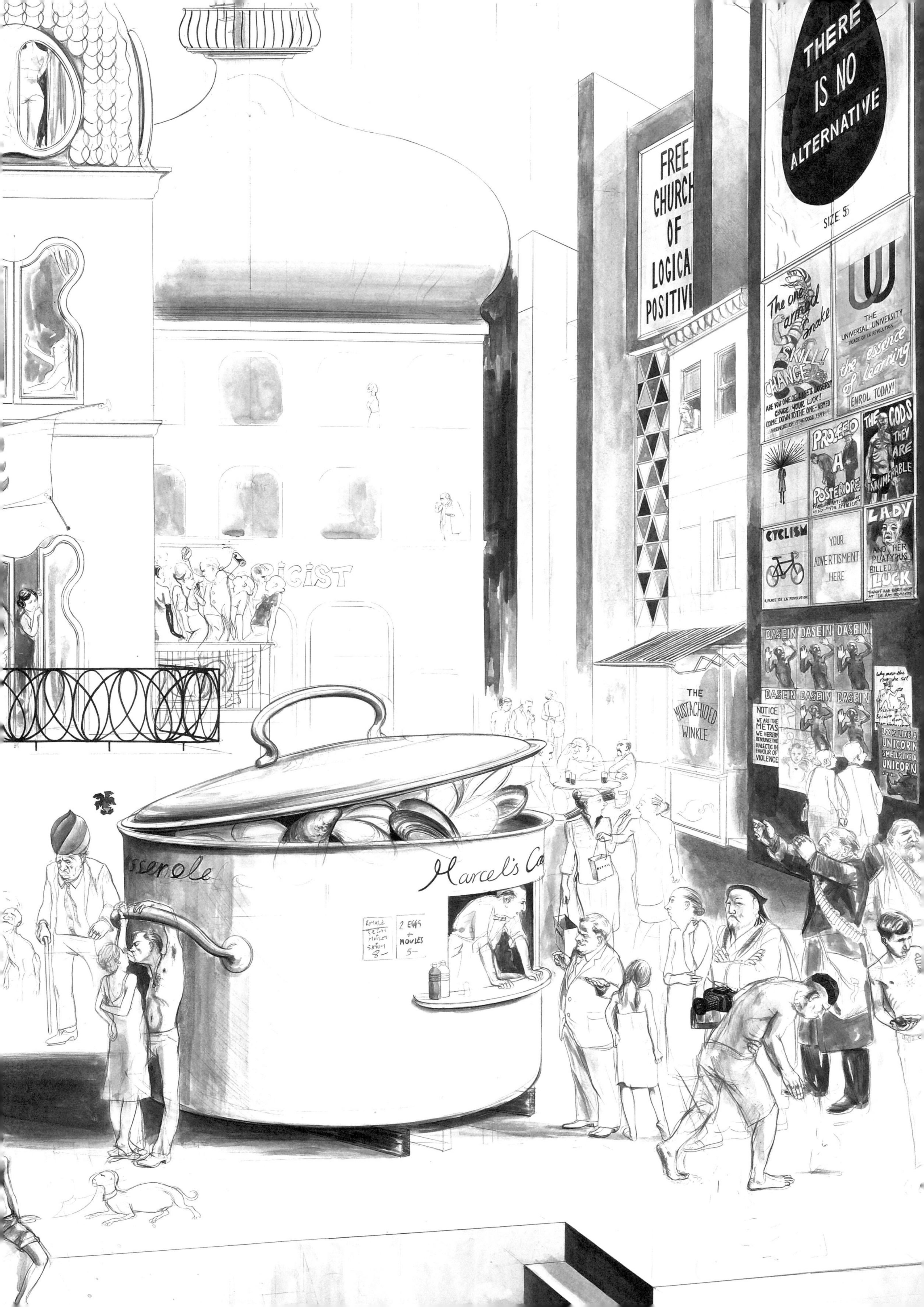

THERE IS NO ALTERNATIVE
SIZE 5
FREE CHURCH OF LOGICA POSITIVI
The one armed Snake
SKILL! CHANGE
THE UNIVERSAL UNIVERSITY
the essence of Learning
ENROL TODAY!
PROCEED A POSTERIORE
THE GODS THEY ARE INNUMERABLE
CYCLISM
YOUR ADVERTISMENT HERE
LADY AND HER PLATYPUS BILLED LUCK
DASEIN DASEIN DASEIN
DASEIN DASEIN DASEIN
NOTICE WE ARE THE METAS WE HEREBY RENOUNCE THE DIALECTIC IN FAVOUR OF VIOLENCE
LOOKS LIKE A UNICORN SMELLS LIKE A UNICORN
THE MUSTACHIOED WINKLE
Marcel's Ca
sserole
2 EGGS + MOULES 5-

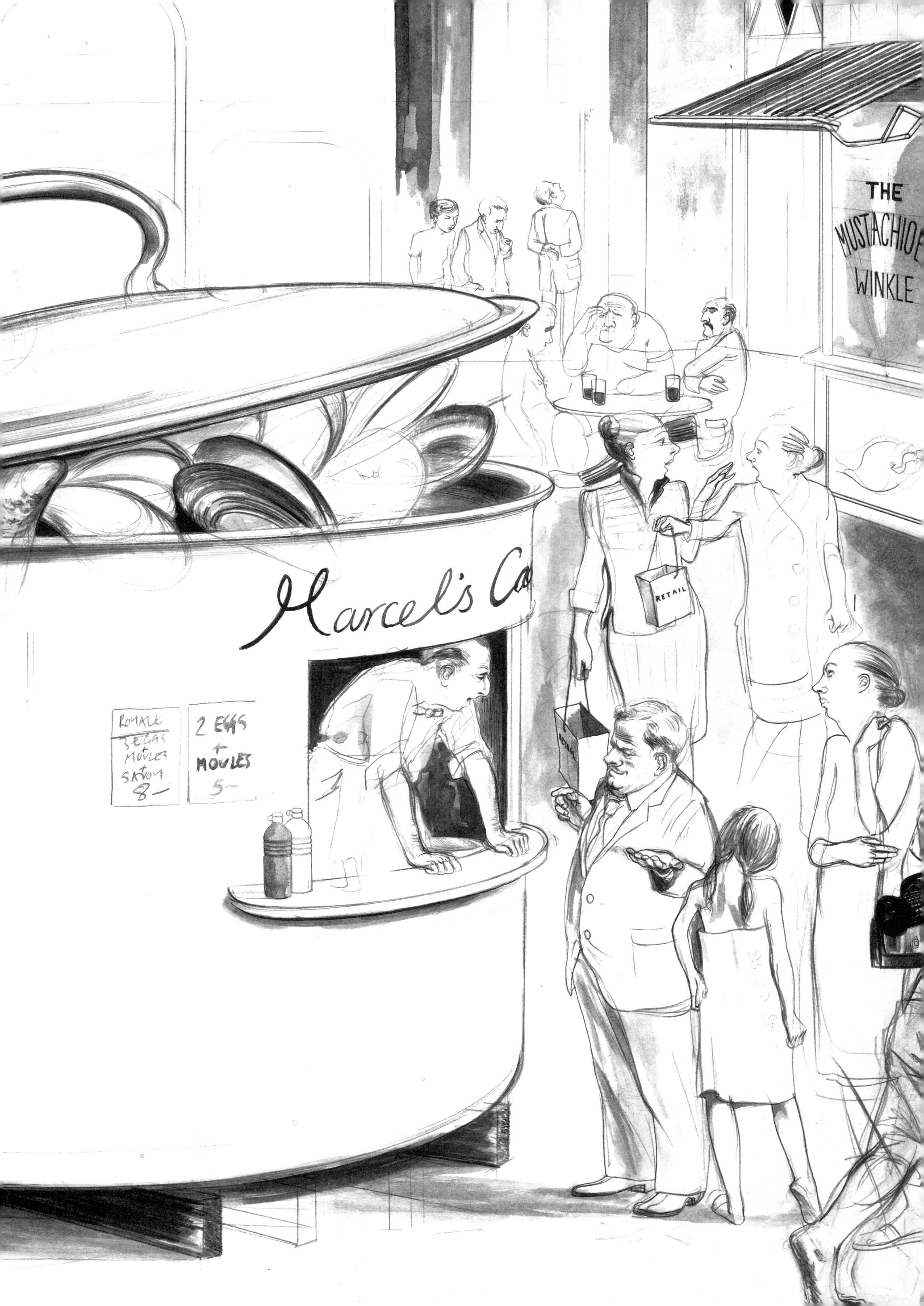
THE
MUSTACHIOE
WINKLE
Marcel's Ca
RETAIL
ROYALE
3 EGGS + MOULES + SAVOY 8—
2 EGGS + MOULES 5—

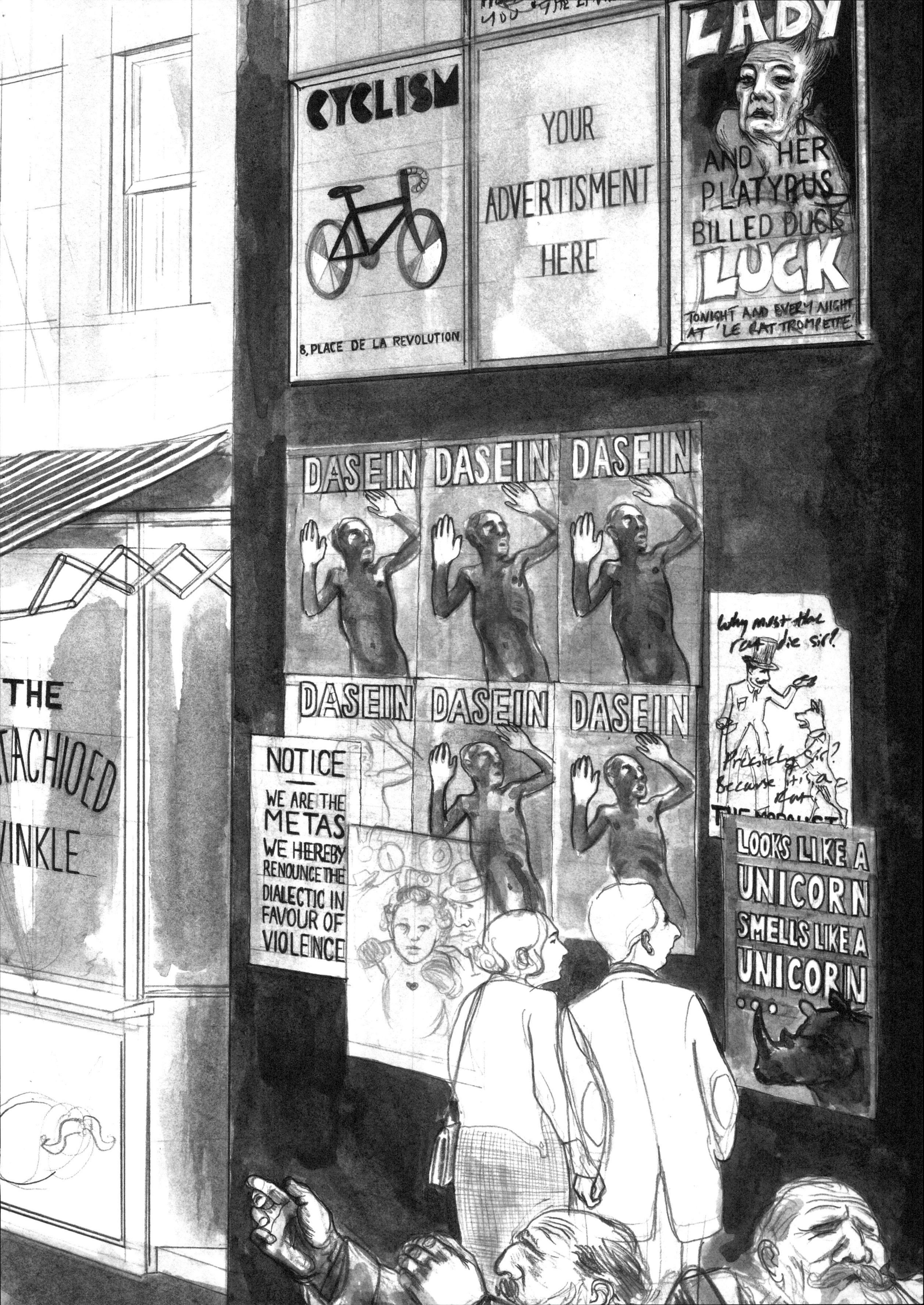
CYCLISM
8, PLACE DE LA REVOLUTION
YOUR ADVERTISMENT HERE
LADY
AND HER PLATYPUS BILLED DUCK
LUCK
TONIGHT AND EVERY NIGHT AT 'LE RAT TROMPETTE'
THE
TACHIOED
WINKLE
DASEIN
DASEIN
DASEIN
DASEIN
DASEIN
DASEIN
Why must the rat die sir?
Precisely sir? Because it is a rat
NOTICE
WE ARE THE METAS
WE HEREBY RENOUNCE THE DIALECTIC IN FAVOUR OF VIOLENCE
LOOKS LIKE A UNICORN
SMELLS LIKE A UNICORN
...

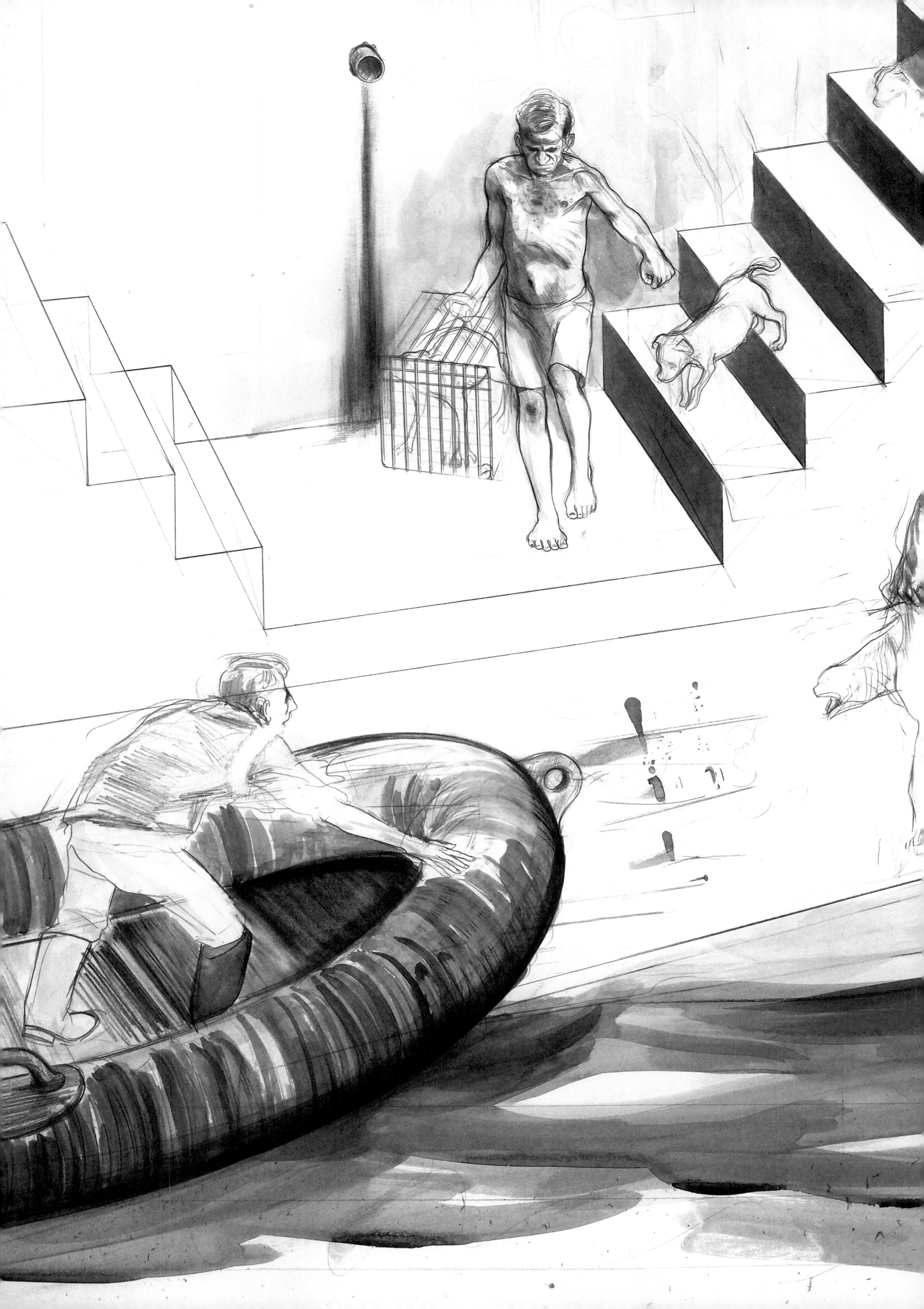

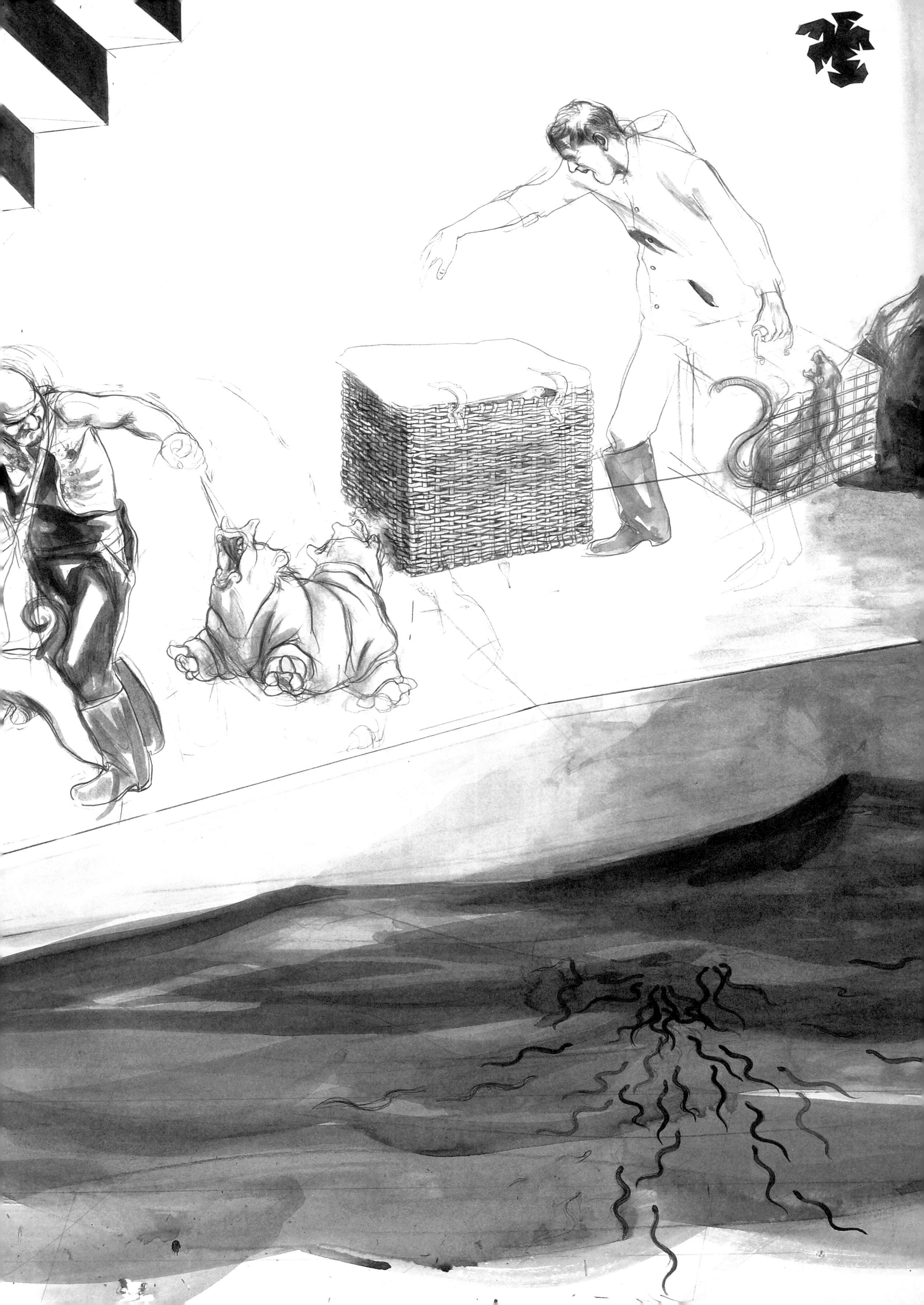

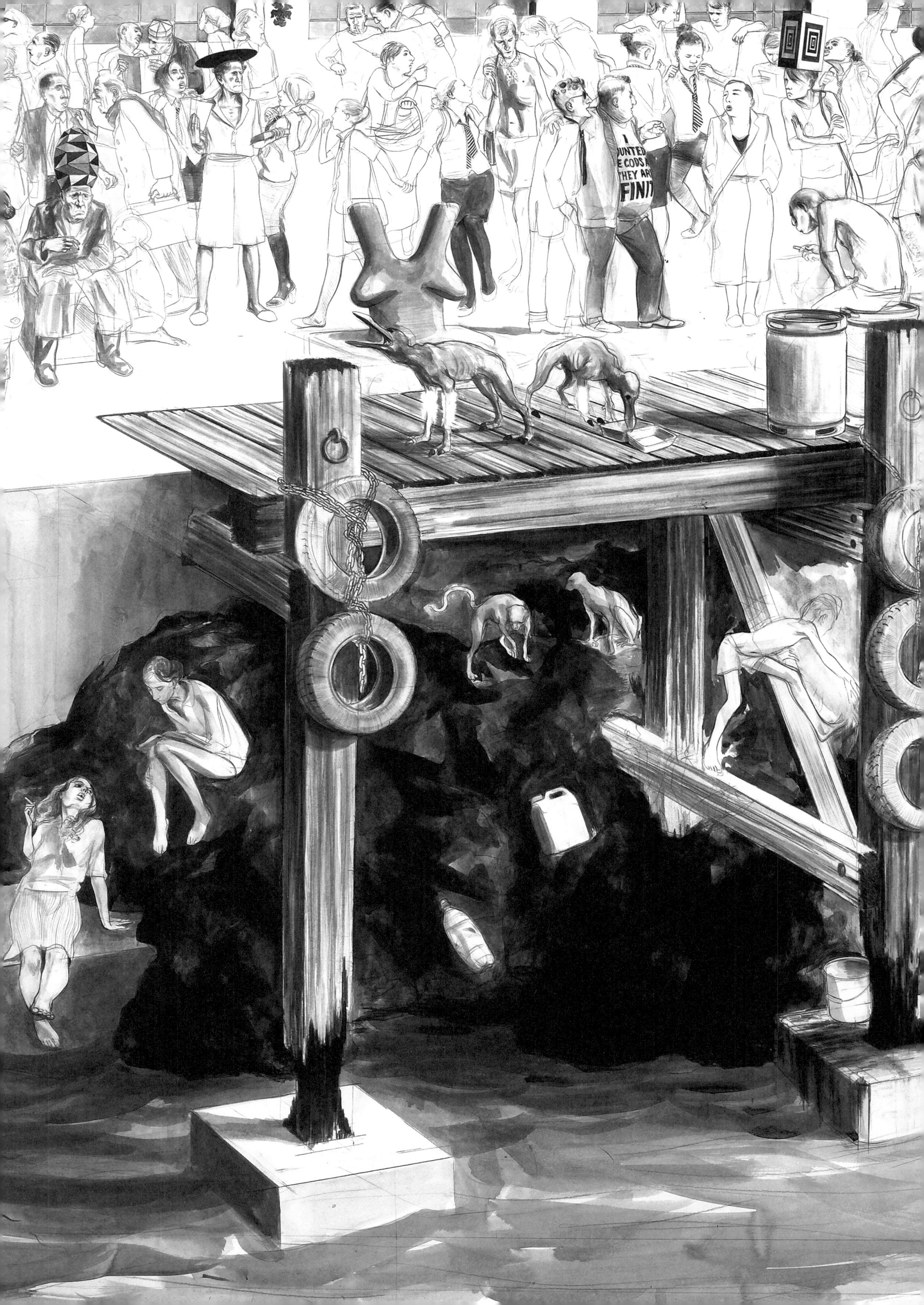
I
UNTED
E GODS A
THEY AR
FINIT

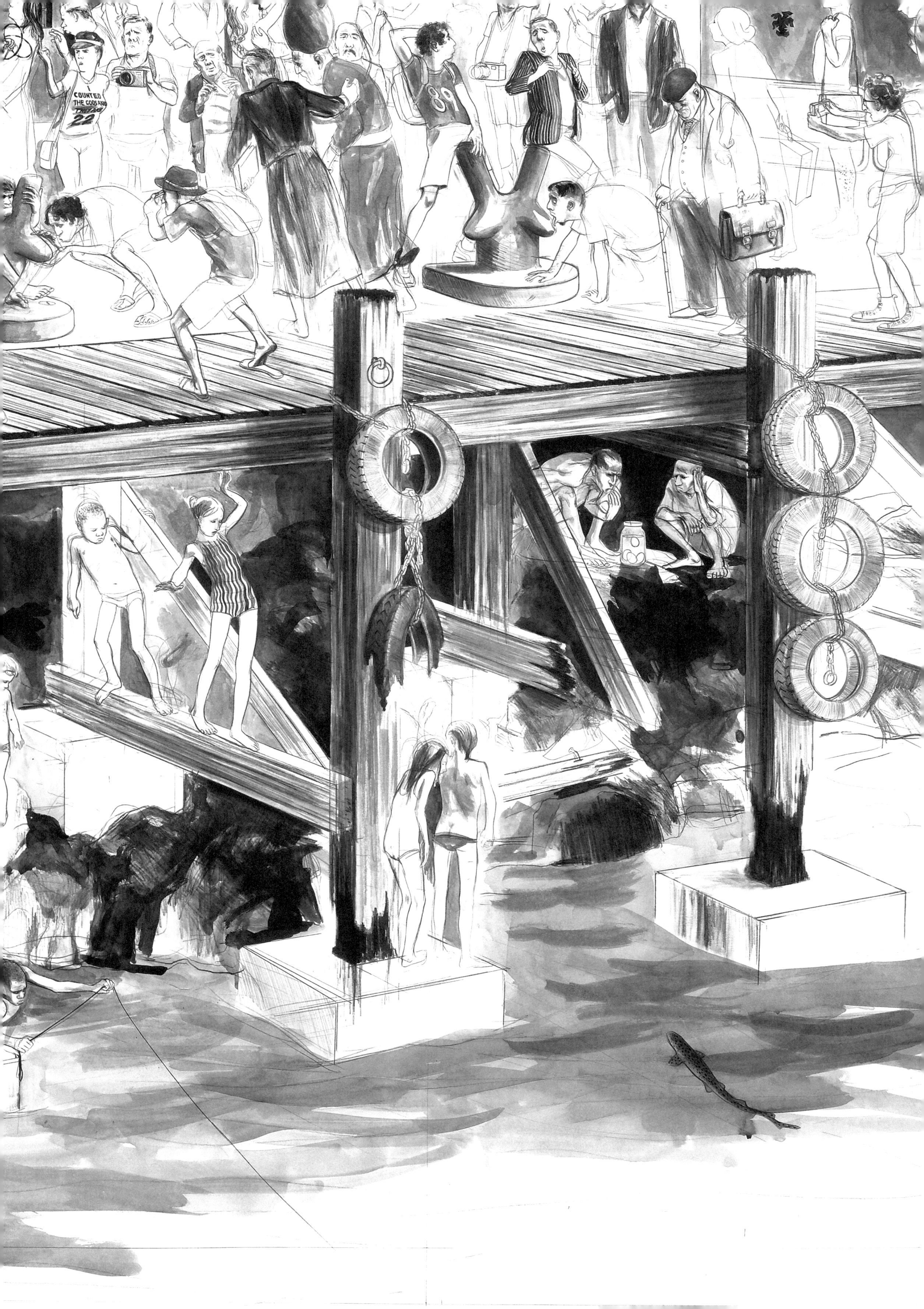
I COUNTED THE GODS AND THEY ARE 22

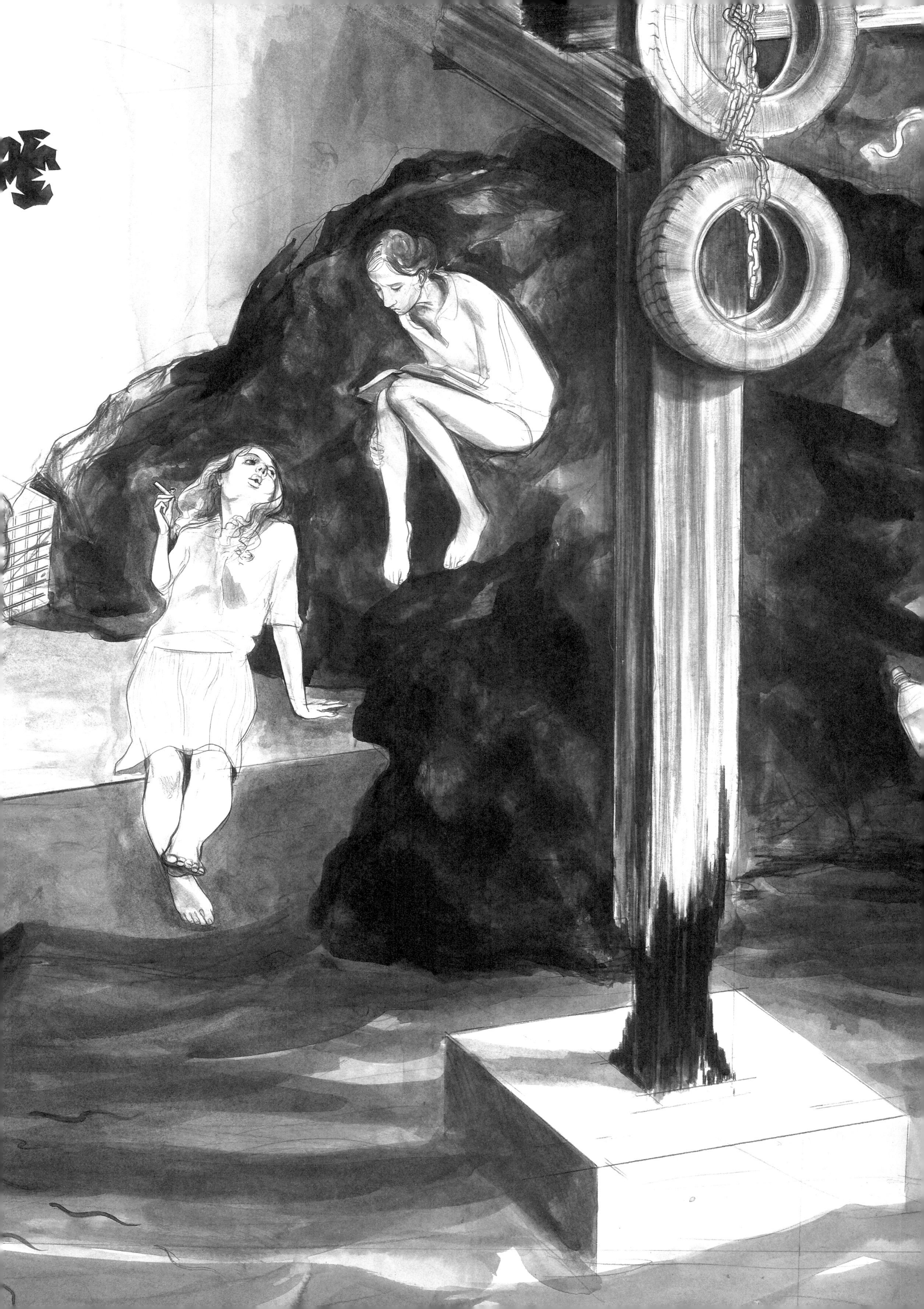

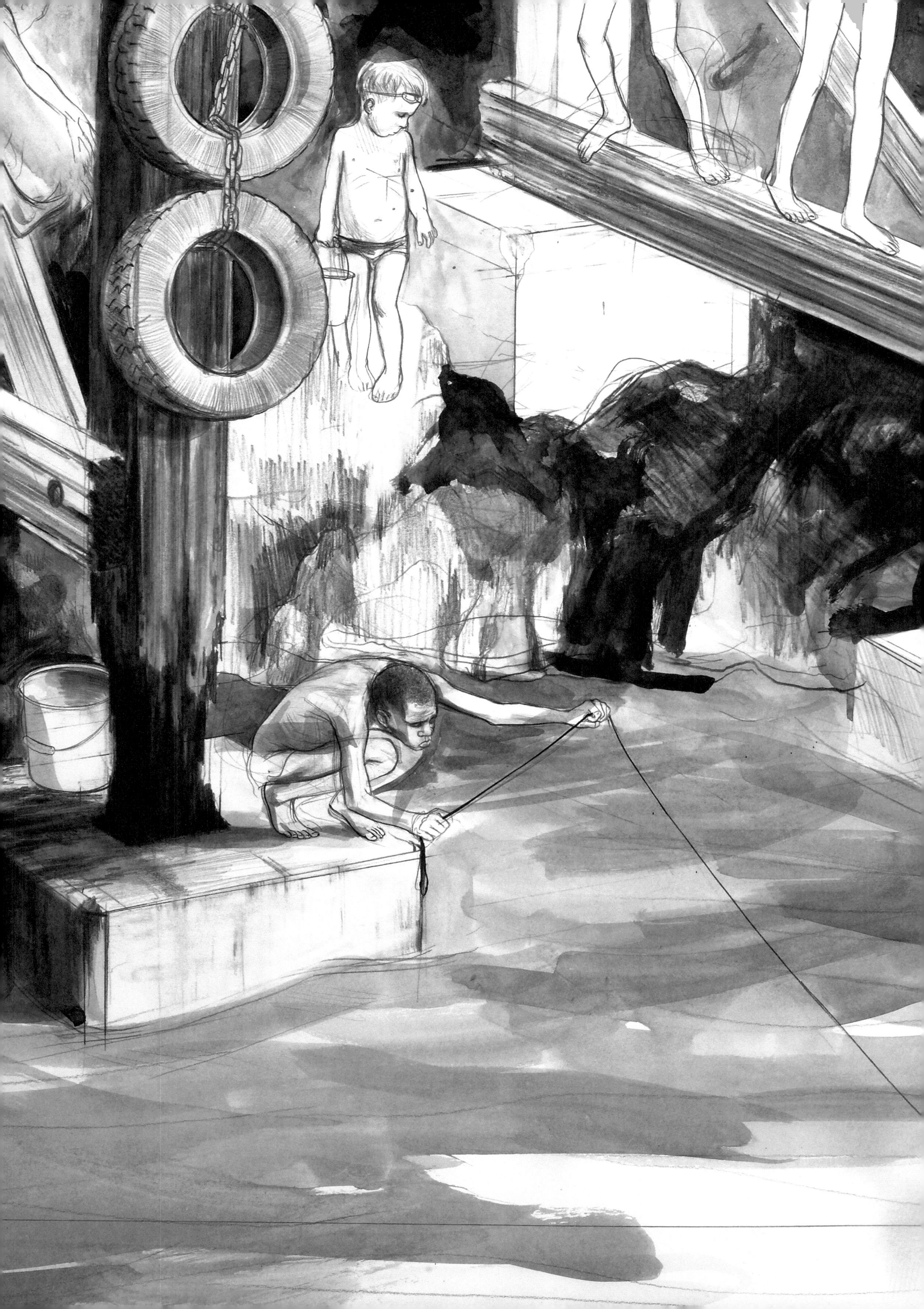

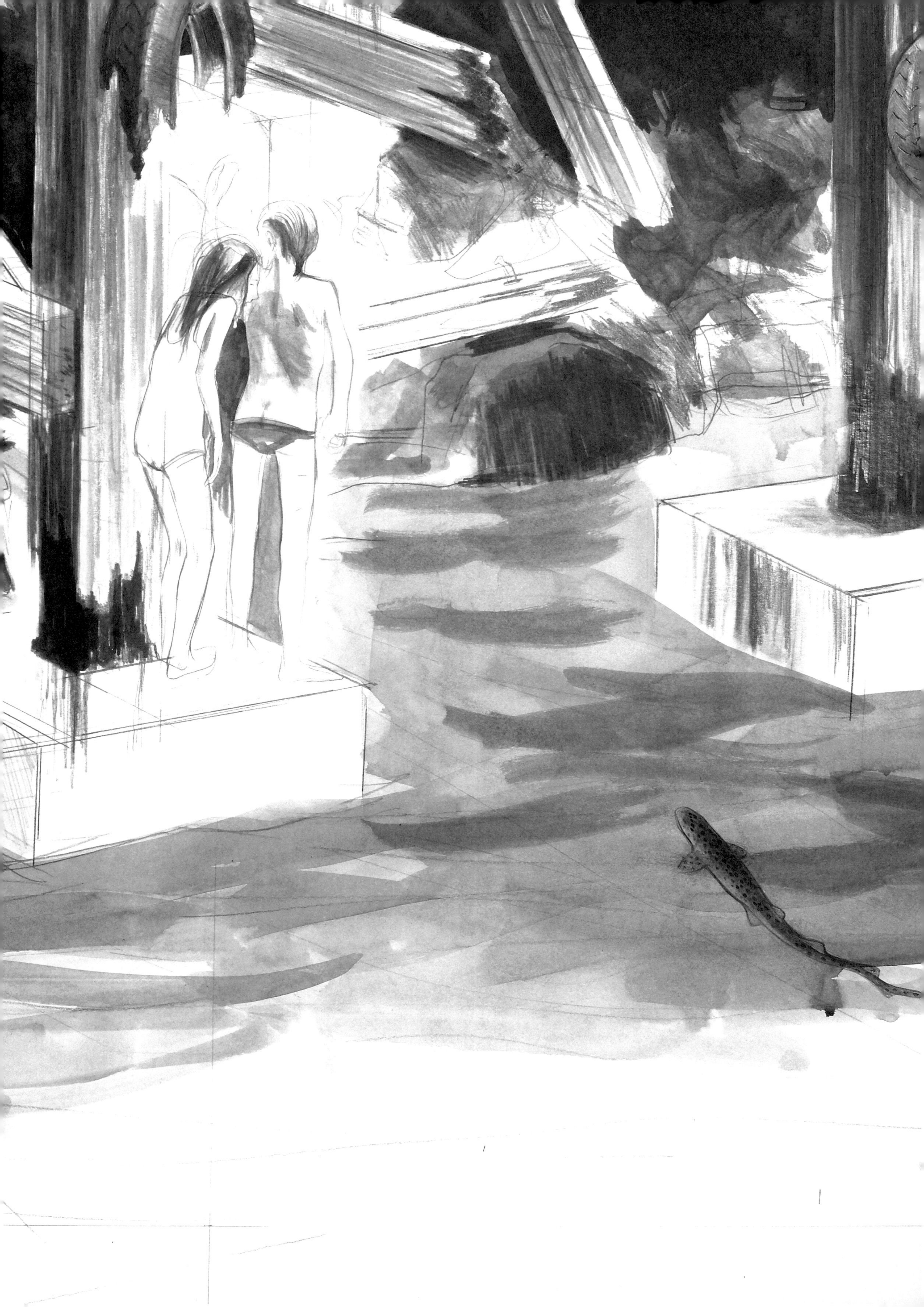

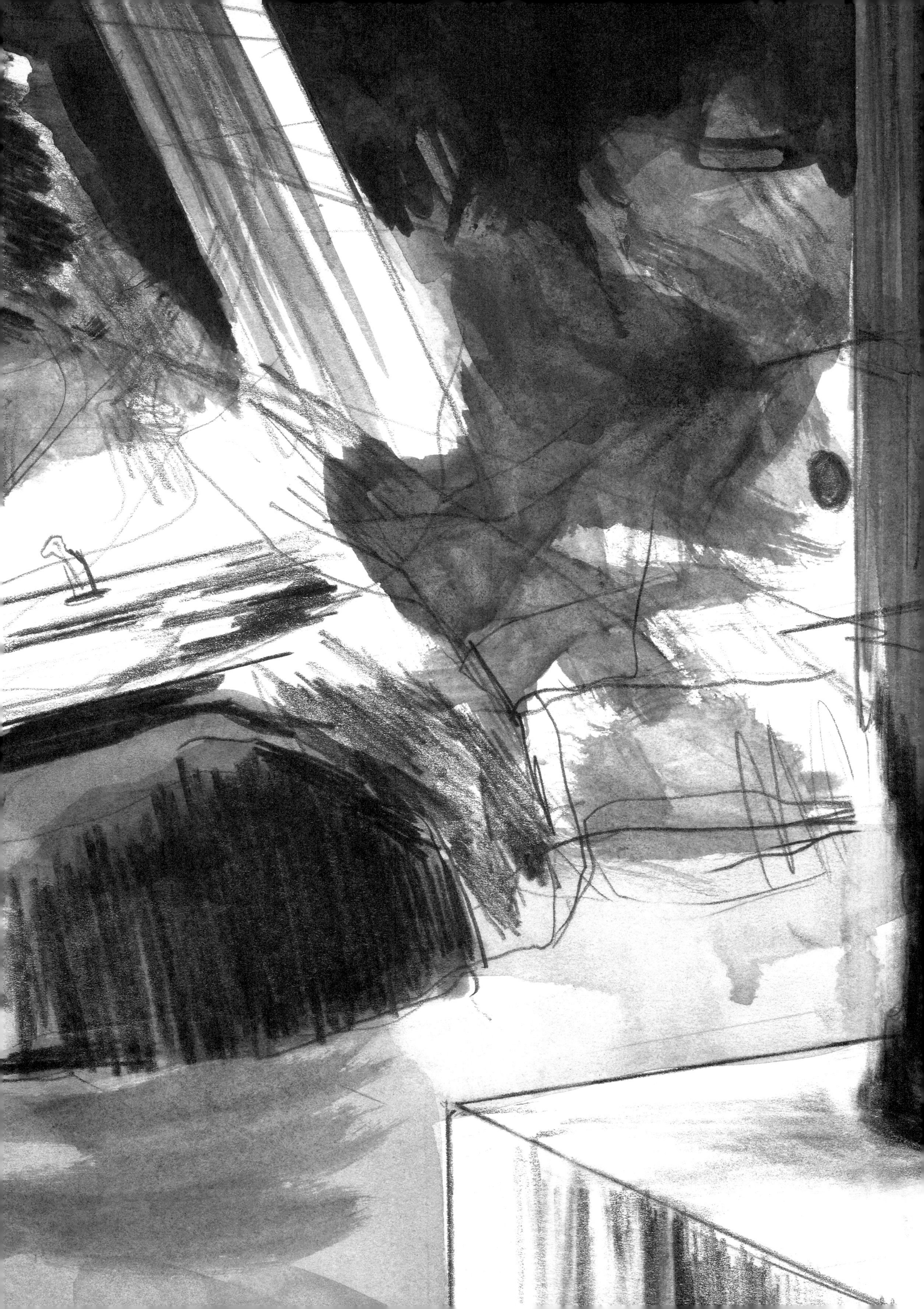

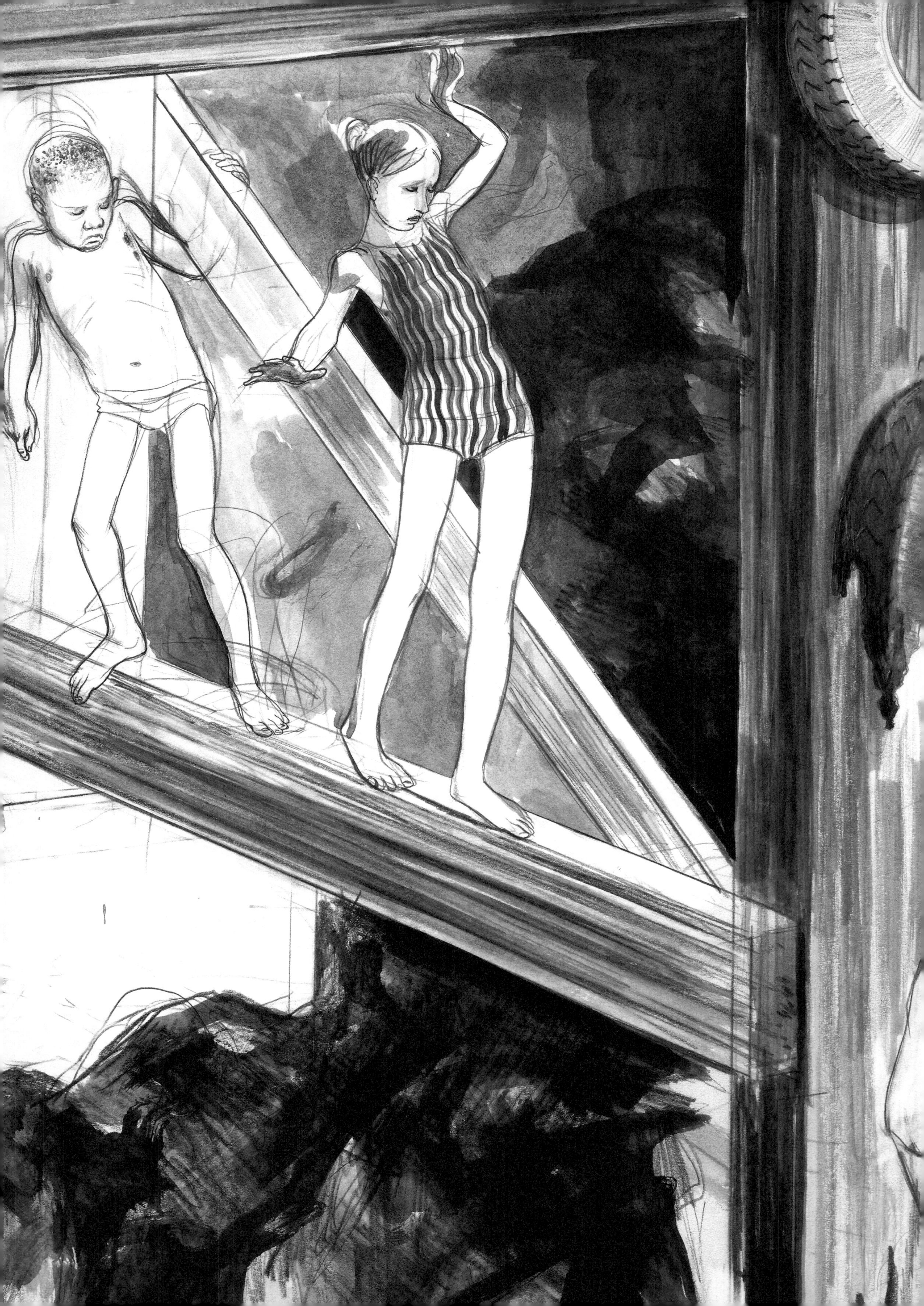

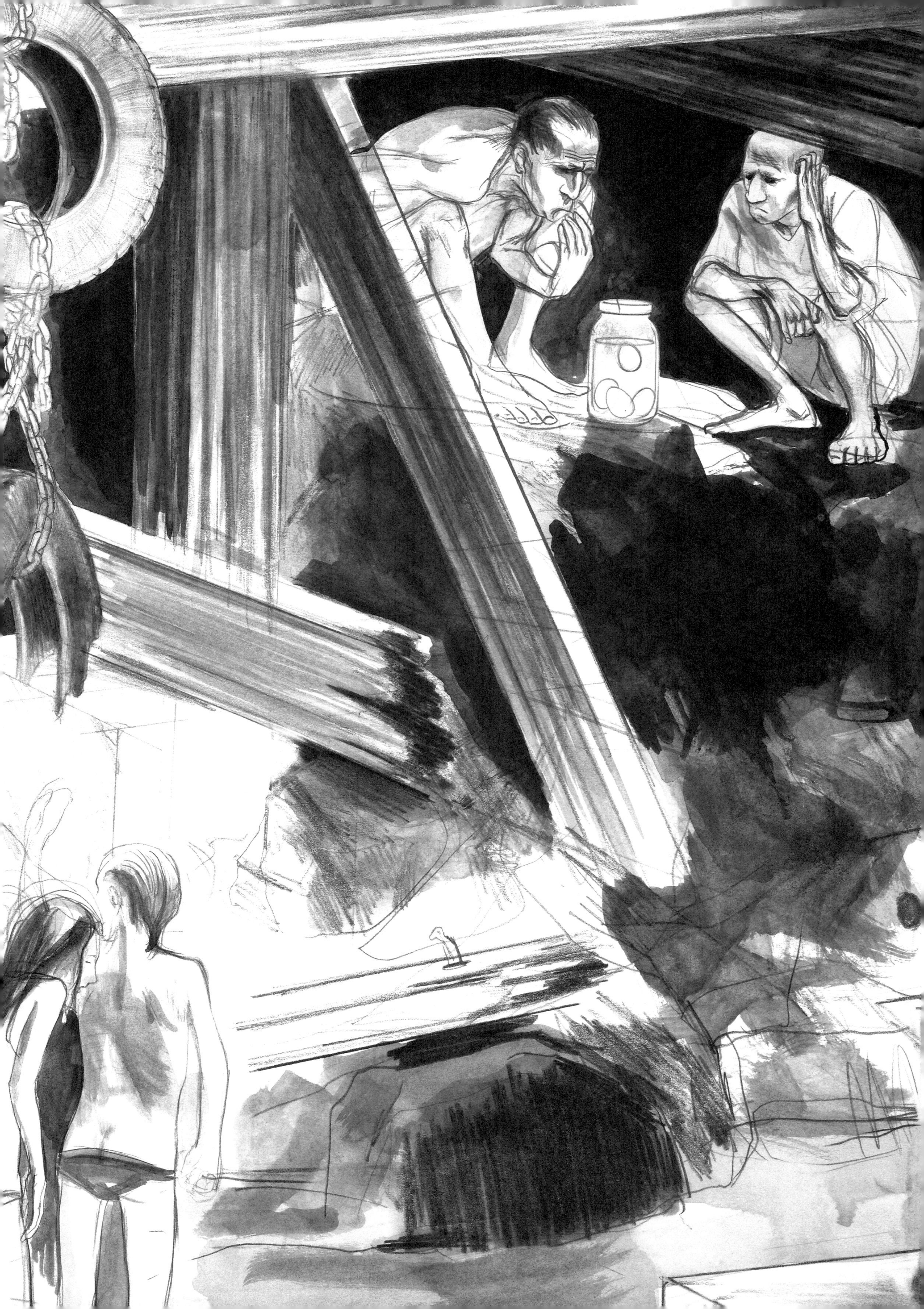

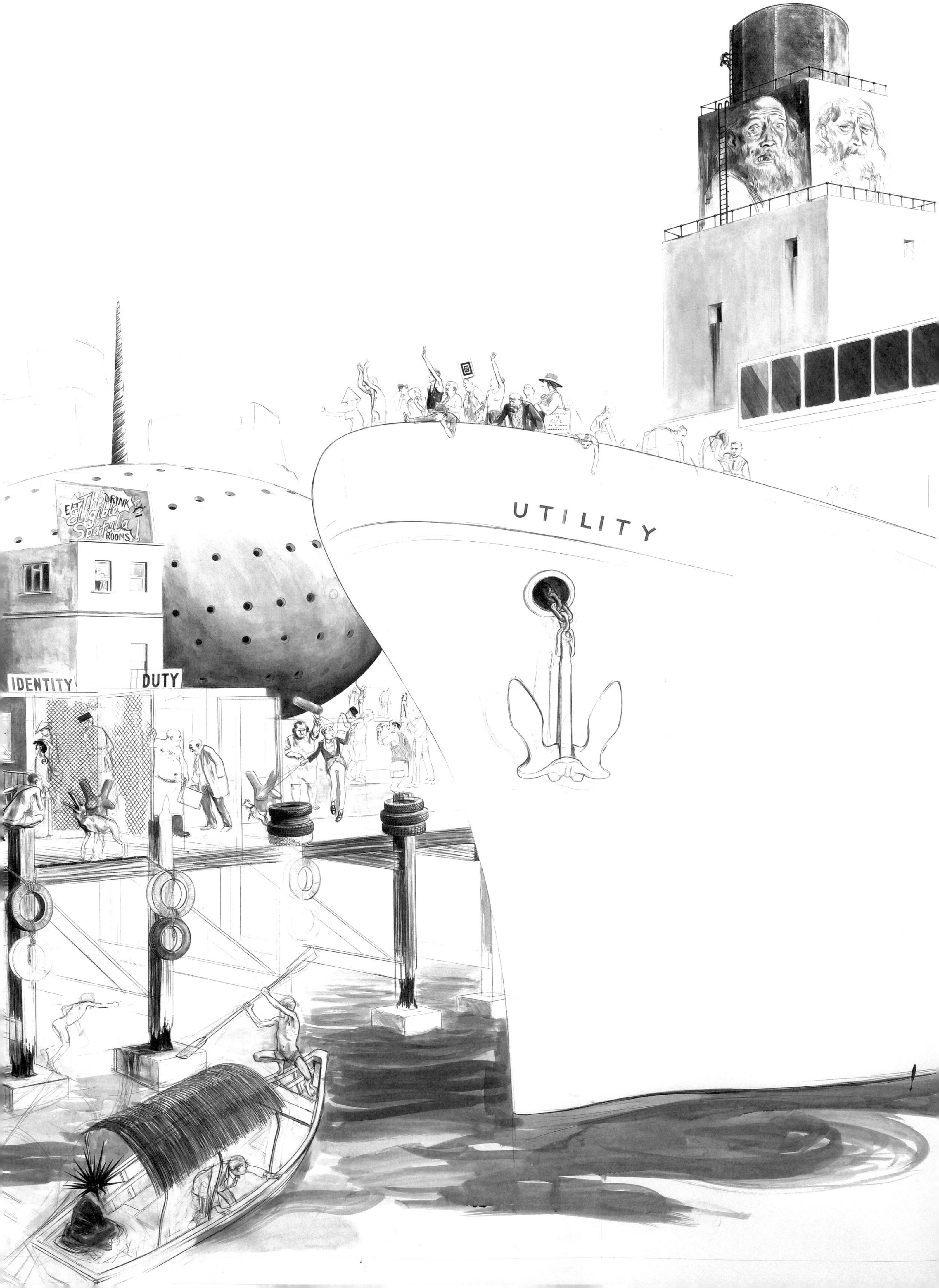
EAT DRINK
The Eligible Spatula
ROOMS
IDENTITY
DUTY
UTILITY

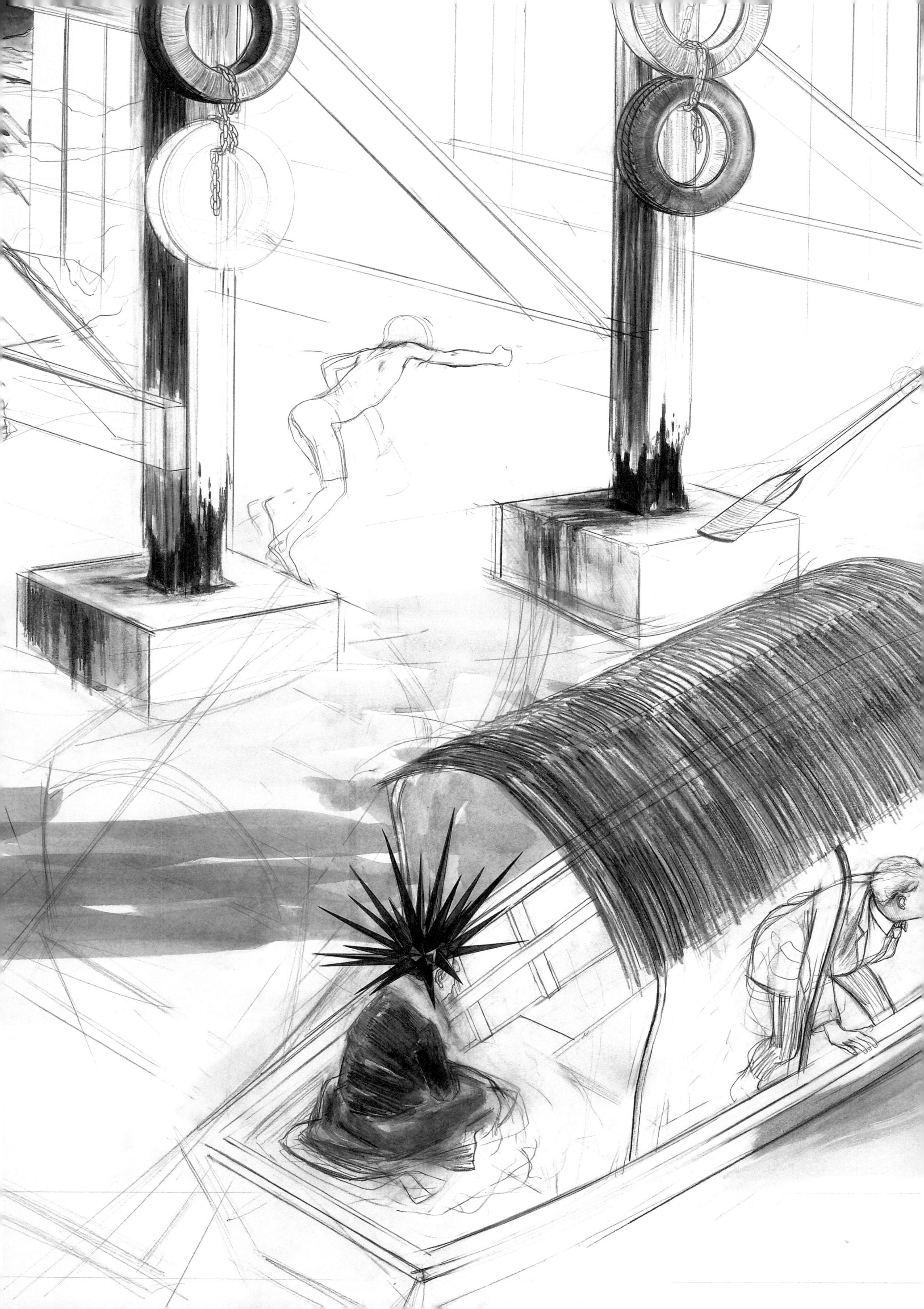

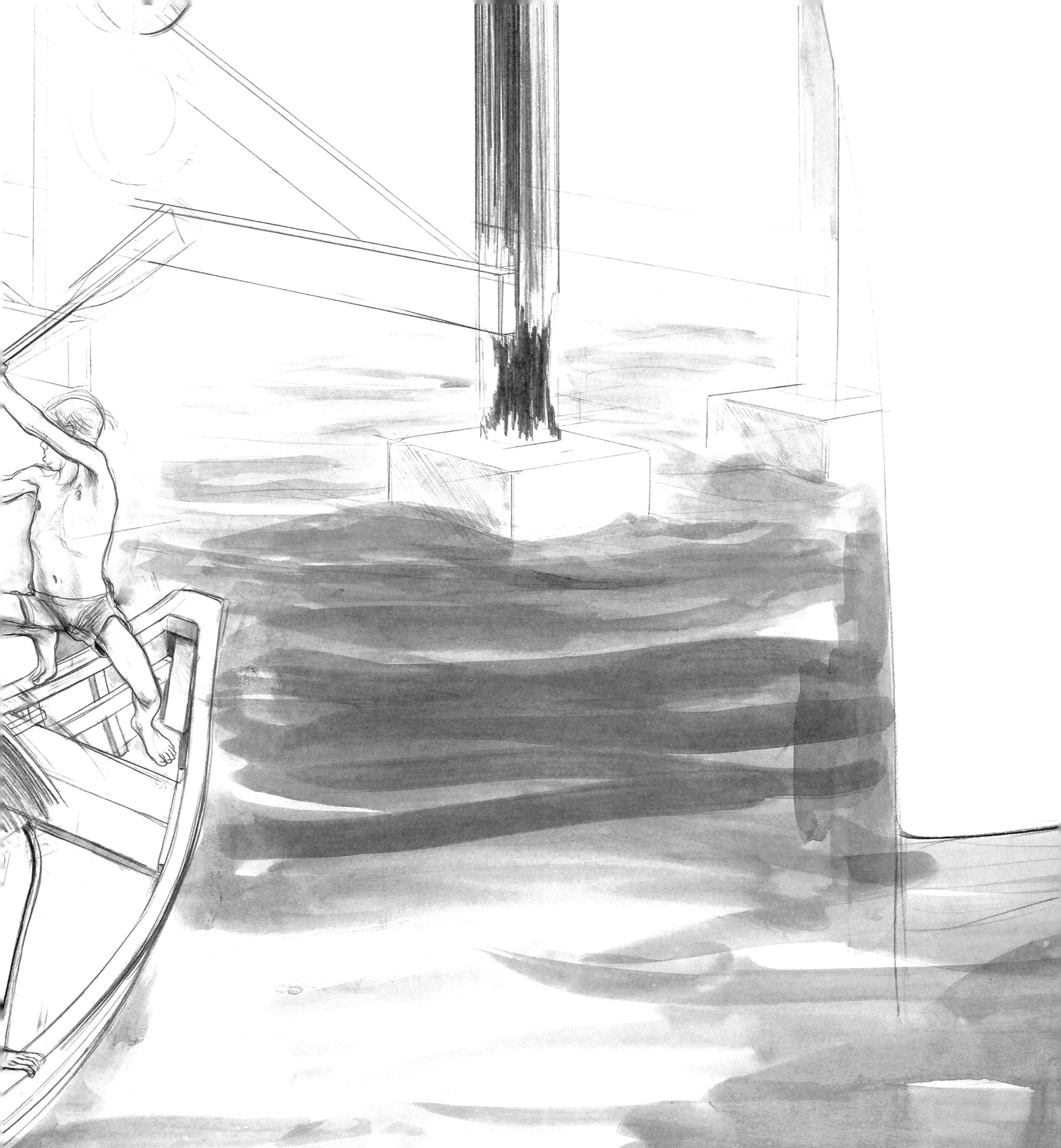

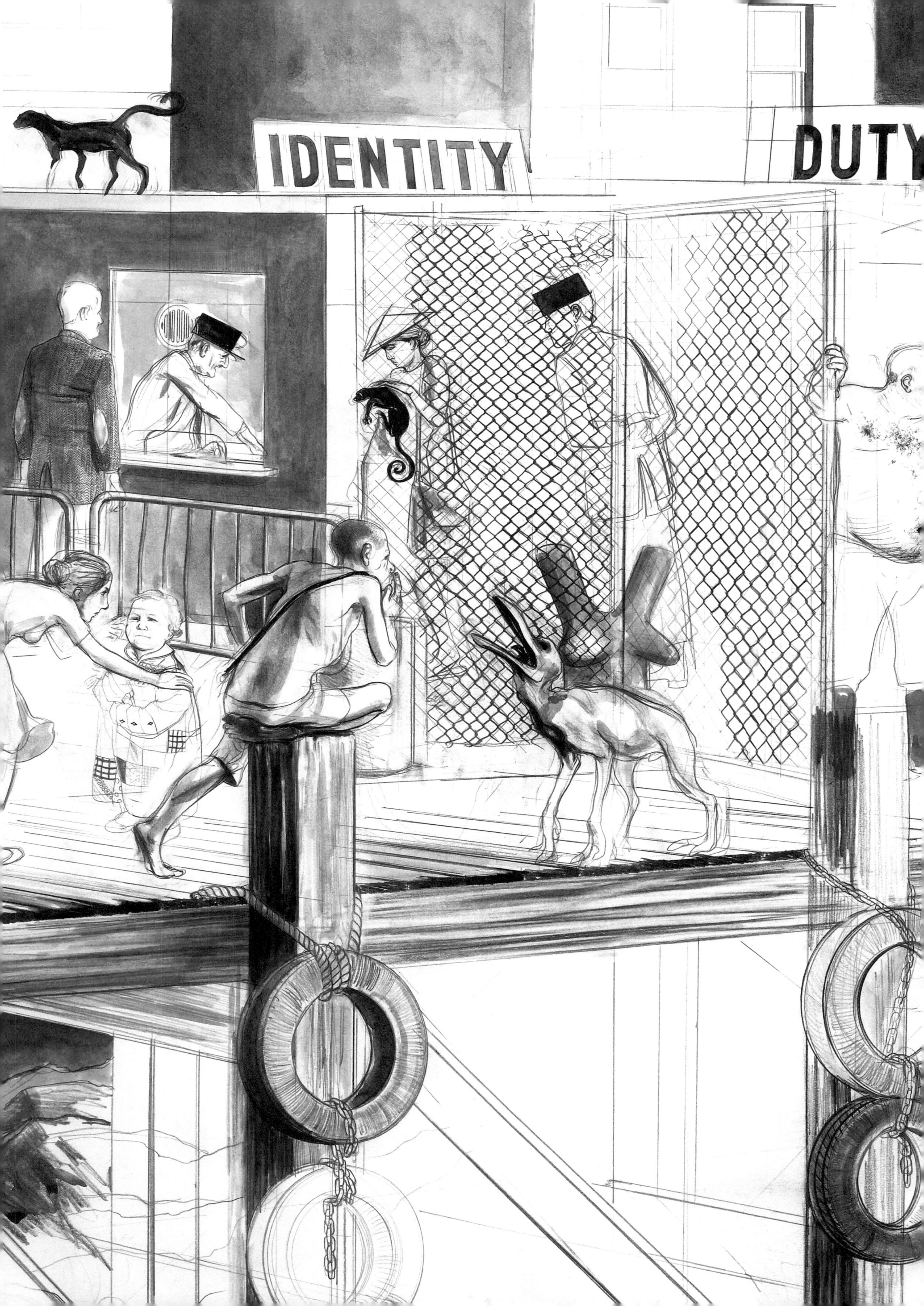
IDENTITY
DUTY

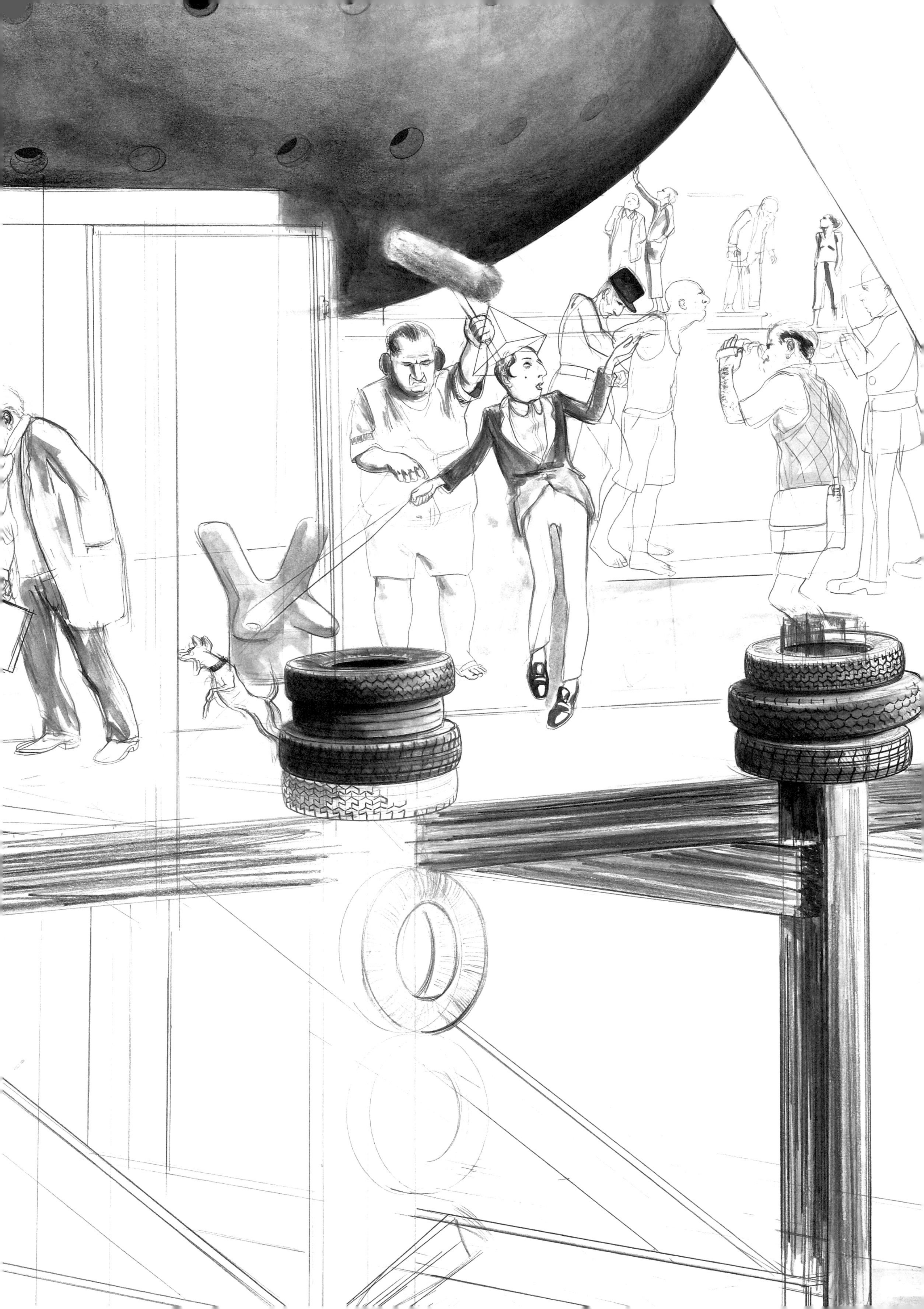

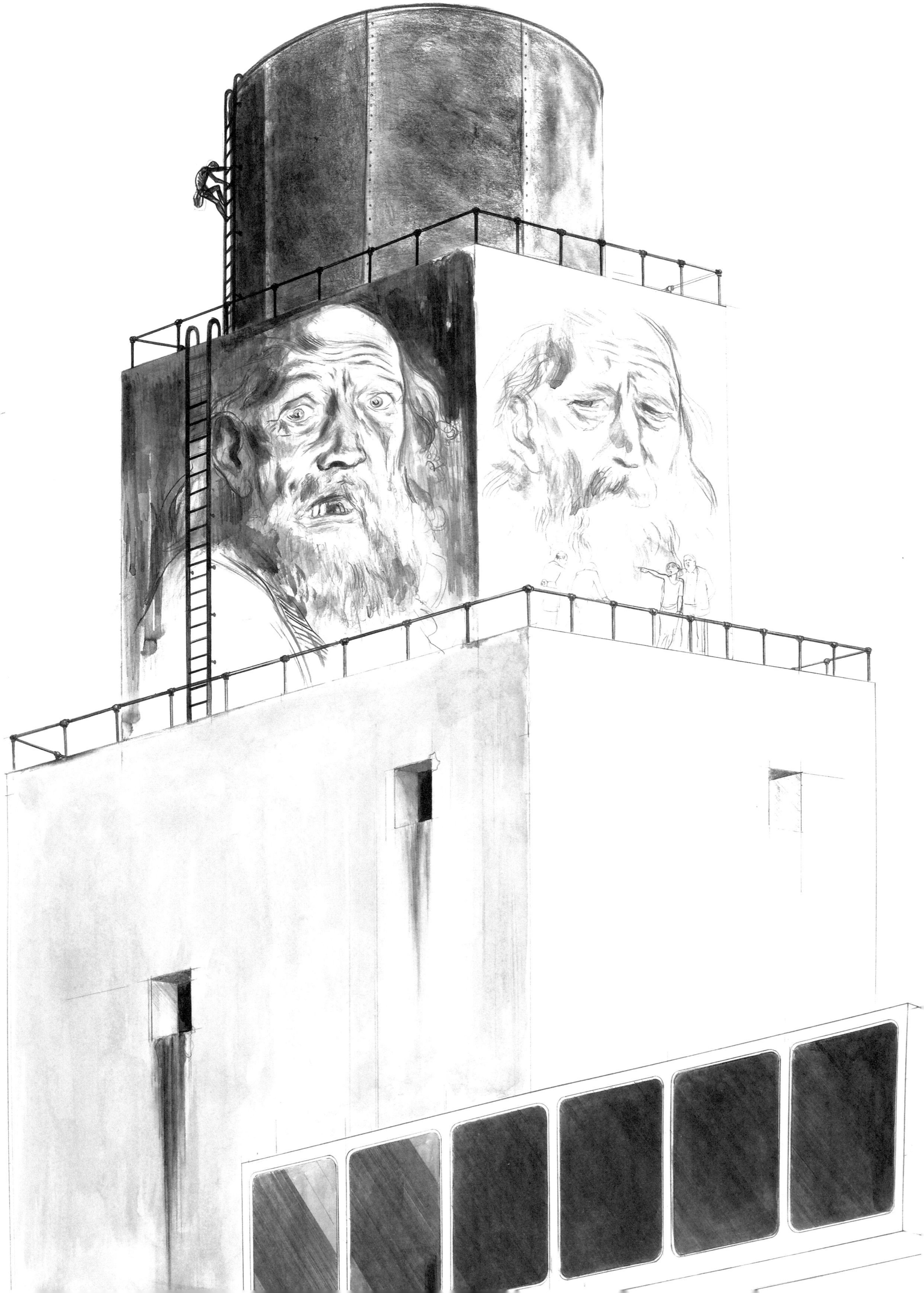

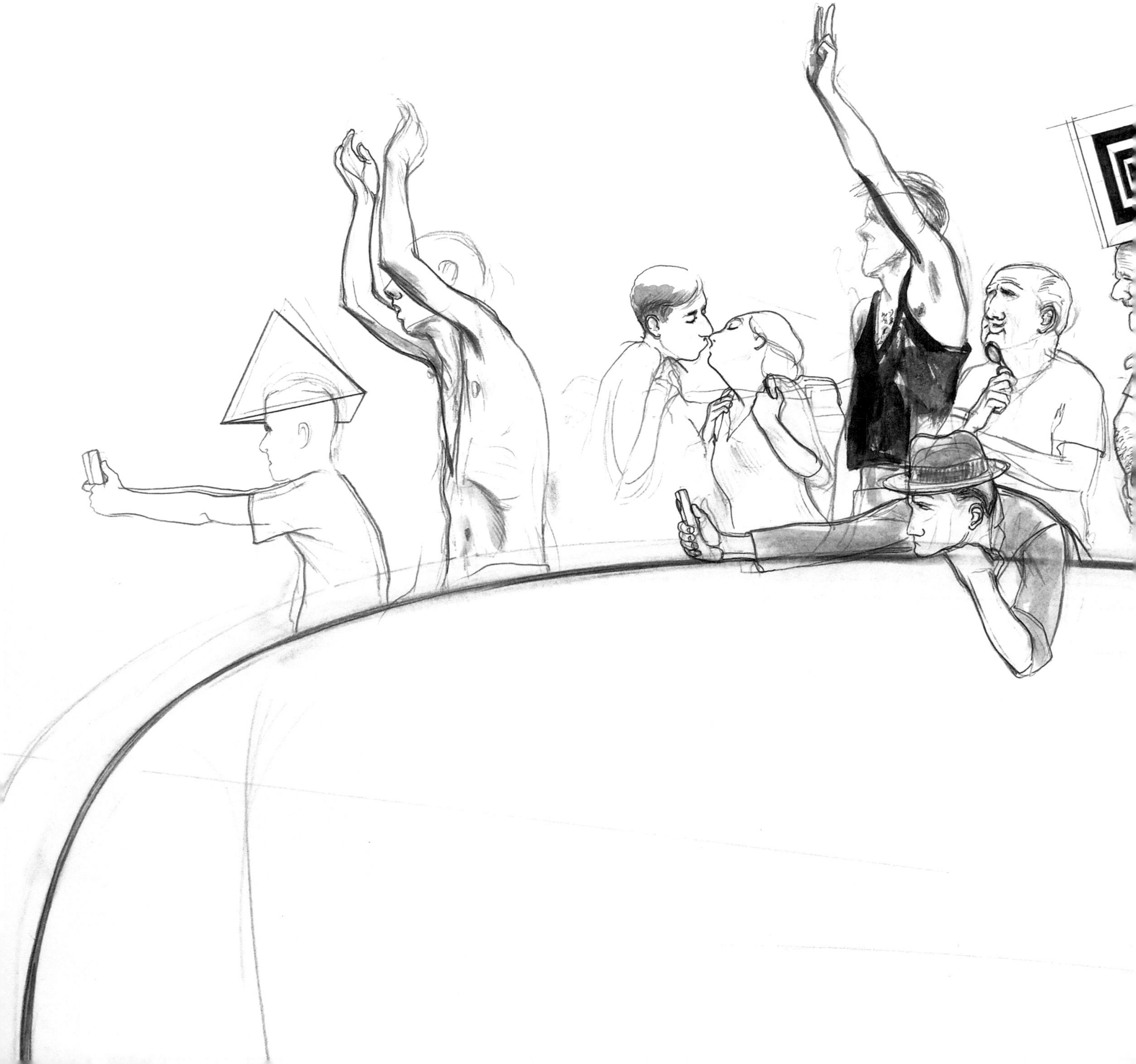

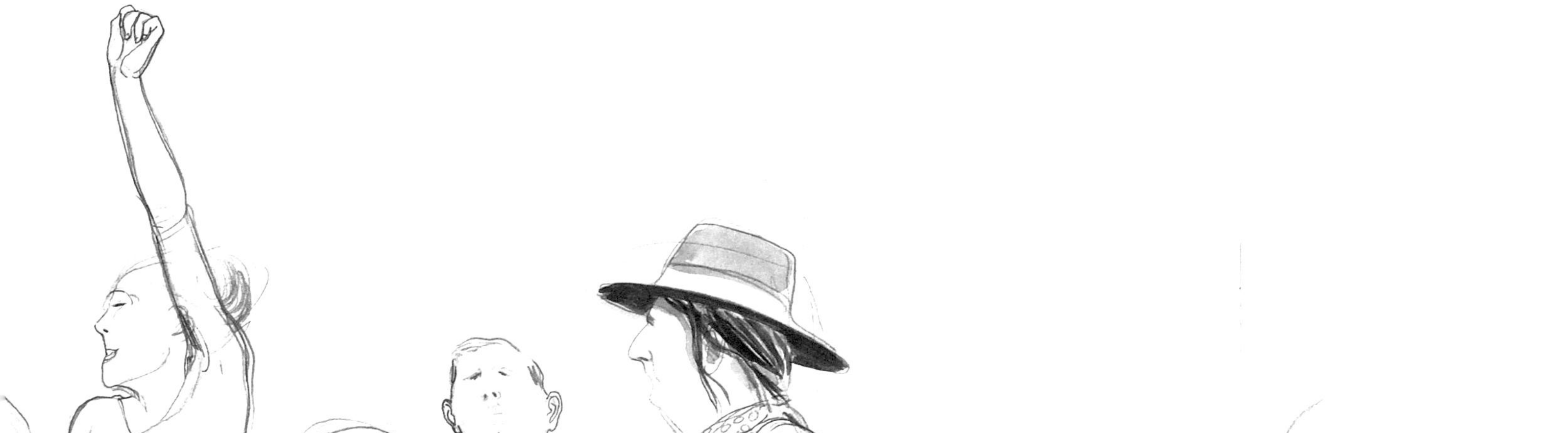
VERYTHING
IS
REAL
2ND BIENNALE
OF
ONOMATOPOEIA

EPILOGUE

This is the plain where Rocco once found a dead monster.

Within its thinness I am profoundly lost.

Multitudes of round white flowers vanish into the endless ring of light on the horizon and there is little else, other than the wind that ruffles the meadows.

Every so often I think I see, at the edge of my vision, some small animal flitting, but I cannot say that any of these sightings are conclusive.

I resolve to fix my eyes downwards and to comb the ground in search of any sign of diversity. A little flat stone ... the remains of a small and long-dead creature ... possibly ... strange S-shaped lines in the dust ... some foamy substance on a stalk ... another stone ... an old plastic bottle! When turned upside down and shaken, it yields some murky liquid that disappears into the ground.

Many have ventured to the remotest part of this far off isle. Some return to tell the story. Those who do say they came in search of something new, for it is the fancy of the hunter that, in this reified atmosphere, a beast called the Noumenon may reside. The existence of this creature has never been proven, yet there is a deep conviction that it must indeed be, and do so here in the wilderness, for the rest of the Island is well charted.

Some come alone so as not to alarm the creature, but hope to enchant it – yet any sighting reported by such solitaries is dismissed as the altitude induced hallucination of the wishful or the fabrication of the charlatan. Others come in pairs so as to have somebody to corroborate their testimonies, but none have been successful. It seems 'three's a crowd' as far as the Noumenon is concerned.

Then there have been great enterprises when hundreds have journeyed up here with dogs and nets and all manner of contraptions and have sought to encircle the creature, fruitlessly. This is clearly a being of infinite finesse. Its existence is sustained by faith alone or, as the *Urbane Wit* commented, "It's behind you!"

Nevertheless, there is an ocean of amnesia that new generations must cross to come to the island, to pull their barks ashore, and to savour the moist air - each expedition with its newest equipment, a picture of jovial young women and men on the beach full of optimism as they head for the darkness.

I too was drawn up here by the scent of this enigmatic cat and am all regret. I would gladly settle for the impression of its droppings if I could be delivered from the situation I now find myself in.

I am disgusted at my weakness of character for I must admit that a sickening loneliness has come upon me more quickly and profoundly than I had imagined it could. I yearn to be planted back in the marginally less lonely situation of the café in the outpost of Onomatopy, where I first conceived this misguided expedition. Where a rude waiter dumped my coffee in front of me, spilling a good deal in the saucer, conducted exclusive banter with the barmen and made lewd comments about inaccessible females (to him through coarseness, to me through shyness) who walked past the window. Where two huge men in tall hats sat strikingly by a mirror on the wall, engrossed in conversation.

A mendicant wandered into the café and mumbled something to me in dialect about milk for his baby (absent) – from which I understood he wished to indent me for currency – and hung around for several seconds after my refusal, allowing me to inhale his hum. I thought, "Drat, why don't the waiters intervene and remove this loon from the premises?". To my discomfort he then took a place at the bar, where he appeared to be on first name terms with the staff, and proceeded to drink a coffee, served to him immaculately, apparently on the house, exchanging friendly salutations with the giants in the corner as he did so.

But I am far from Onomatopy and I don't know my way back, indeed death is closer than town.

Yesterday I saw that pretentious hare at a distance. It stopped a moment and looked in my direction, I thought in pity. I hoped it might point the direction home, but instead it just flashed its rings at me and passed on. As an afterthought I fumbled a couple of cartridges into my gun, but the hare was long gone.

Another hunter once told me that all you really amount to out here is the contents of your bag, the contents of yourself, and your gun. You have to concentrate to remember what you are, which is why I have started to write, to help me remember. It's no good just thinking; you have to think, "I am thinking!"

Each day – a subtle event at these latitudes – I make an inventory to keep me together, or rather to keep myself apart from things:

Self: I am called Only McFew (really!). My best friend is a girl – I call her Miss Miss. I am in love with her but she has no idea, or pretends not to notice. I am a man.

Bag: Two pencils. One notebook. One jar. A knife, naturally, with which to skin that blasted hare when it gets too bold. Half a bag of dried banana slices. One one-armed snake. I'll put it with the other one I have at home, if I ever make it back. I'll mount them on L-shaped bits of wood and have them as bookends. That's a cheering thought. One hole-punch, the cherished possession of Miss Miss, which she lent me a while ago (a burdensome piece of equipment and utterly useless in my current circumstances). I have it with me because I forgot to take it out of my bag before I left and did not notice the weight due to my jaunty attitude at the outset of the expedition.

My thoughts turn to an erotic meditation on Miss Miss.

I know I must be high up the world for the flowers are vivid against the dark grey sky and I hear the noises without causes, tiny musical explosions in the air – a phenomenon which must be perceived to be believed, like flying fish, of which I have heard sailors speak (and whom I don't believe).

I feel as though I am walking sideways through time - my past to the left of me, my future to the right. I cannot carry on this way. I must make a choice but won't for fear of it being the wrong one. I am just continuing, putting one foot in front of the other, hoping for a sign to direct me.

Meanwhile, worst of all, I have started to doubt. I seriously doubt the Noumenon and wonder if I have jeopardized my life, sacrificed my bones to the anonymous dust of the plain, all for the sake of a chimera (I imagine that hare will gingerly approach my corpse when it is sure I am dead beyond the point of resurrection and, when the flesh has rotted from my fingers, it will take my garnet ring for its collection).

I doubt the affections of Miss Miss, or that her fatalist self will view my demise as anything other than the course of events.

Certain other things have also begun to disturb me: sometimes the flowers don't quite align with their stalks. Why have I never seen the bottom of a mountain? Despite my patient efforts in studying the If'enish language, I have acquired no more than a few words, leaving me to suspect that this argot amounts to little more than gobbledygook improvised for the consumption of the tourists.

And finally I have started to wonder if, beyond the shops and bars and lights of Onomatopy, beyond the Plane of the Gods, where the defunct machines and litter are strewn, underneath the mountains and the flowers and the dust and the bones of the hunters, there is an Island at all?

ADDENDA

This book has been produced on the occasion of Charles Avery's exhibition entitled *Onomatopoeia: part 1* at Le Plateau / Frac Île-de-France, Paris; the Kunstverein Hannover; and EX3, Florence.

Since 2005 Charles Avery has been working on an epically structured body of work that evinces – through drawings, objects, installations, and texts – a fictional Island.
The Island, which has no other name, is positioned at the centre of a spiraling archipelago of innumerable smaller islands, inundated by a black ocean. Our knowledge of this *terra incognita* comes via the testimony of a young man – whose name we also never learn – who lands on a remote coast of the Island, believing himself to be its discover, but who is soon disabused of this conceit by a young woman he meets on the shore, and is forced to radically rethink his *raison d'être*.

The Islanders can be understood in many ways: as a meditation on the central themes of philosophy, a critique of all the great dualities, such as the conscious and the subconscious, the real and the unreal, 1 and 2, or as a metaphor for the colonial-style carve up and ownership of the world of ideas.

In 2008 Parasol unit in London hosted the first major exhibition of the project, simply entitled *The Islanders: an introduction* which toured to the Gallery of Modern Art, Edinburgh, and the Museum Boijmans van Beuningen, Rotterdam. That exhibition, and the accompanying book, sought to describe the most important features of the Island, as well as offering an insight into the project, as 'work in progress' as well as amounting to a statement of the ambition and scope for the future of the endeavor. Since that time the focus of the project has moved on to a detailed exploration of the only town on the Island, called Onomatopoeia: a one time colonial outpost, turned boomtown, turned thriving trade centre, turned depression hit slum, turned regenerated tourist destination.

The exhibitions at le Plateau / Frac Île-de-France, Paris; the Kunstverein Hannover; and EX3, Florence are the first major presentations of this important phase of the project, as well as being the first solo institutional shows of the artist's work, in France, Germany and Italy respectively.

This book is dedicated to a single, very large drawing (measuring 2.4 meters in heights, and over 5 meters in lengths) of the port at Onomatopoeia. The point of arrival and departure to and from this fictional realm, it is a focal point of the town, and the Island, and perfectly encapsulates the project as a whole.

The directors of the institutions would like to thank Charles Avery for his extraordinary commitment to the exhibitions and the publication, Marc Kappeler for the graphic design of the catalogue, and the galleries doggerfisher, Edinburgh, Pilar Corrias, London and Sonia Rosso, Turin for their organizational and financial support.

For their facilitation of the project at the individual exhibition venues, Le Plateau / Frac Île-de-France, Paris thanks to the Conseil régional d'Île-de-France, the Ministry of Culture and Communication – Direction régionale des affaires culturelles and the Ville de Paris. The Kunstverein Hannover thanks the Ministry for Science and Culture of the State of Lower Saxony, the NORD / LB, and the Stiftung Horizonte. EX3 would like to thank the Comune di Firenze and the Project Toscanaincontemporanea of the Regione Toscana.

Xavier Franceschi
Director, Le Plateau / Frac Île-de-France, Paris

René Zechlin
Director, Kunstverein Hannover

Sergio Tossi
Director, EX3, Florence

Ma première venue sur l'île remonte à la fin de la grande ruée vers l'algue, sans en avoir bien conscience sur le moment. J'abordai cette terre en pensant être le premier à la découvrir.

J'accostai le rivage isolé à bout de force, épuisé d'avoir dû me battre contre la marée, contre la pluie et contre les paquets d'algues marines qui enserraient mes rames.

Je déposai mon sac à terre avant d'adosser mon fusil à un rocher. Je me mis à peler une banane.

Impossible de distinguer la moindre chose au loin, en raison de l'obscurité et des énormes gouttes de pluie qui venaient m'inonder les yeux. Aussi tendis-je l'oreille. J'écoutai le varech bercé par la houle, le crépitement de l'ondée sur l'argile, ainsi que les craquements et les hululements de bêtes inconnues.

En entamant une autre banane, je commençai à m'imaginer l'accueil que l'on me ferait à mon retour à Triangland : les drapeaux agités sur le quai, l'interview dans la revue *Fancy That,* le message du gouvernement.

C'est en savourant ce sentiment de réussite absolue que je remarquai du coin de l'œil quelque chose qui remuait. J'aperçus en tournant la tête une Souris de Pierre, moitié animale, moitié minérale, qui tentait de se dissimuler parmi les rochers.
Son cœur ne bat qu'une fois tous les mille ans, et le moindre de ses mouvements est semblable à une contorsion atroce.
Je pensai alors ramener chez moi cette curiosité en souvenir du nouveau monde, pour la montrer au Premier Ministre.
Je sortis donc un vieux bocal à cornichon de mon sac pour tenter de l'y déposer avec un peu de son environnement moite.
La pluie tombait plus drue à présent ; des ténèbres émanaient d'horribles bruissements qui semblaient se rapprocher. Je tentai de les ignorer.

Cependant, en refermant le couvercle, un autre son plus familier me fit tressaillir : celui de l'Humanité.

En m'avançant dans les terres, je distinguai une pâle figure qui s'approchait de moi sur le rivage : une jeune femme tenant un panier, qui sautait de rocher en rocher et se parlait apparemment à elle-même. Elle portait une chemise à l'ourlet trempé et crotté, un petit gilet et des bottes de pluie. Comme intriguée par certaines herbes, elle s'arrêtait de temps à autre parmi les rochers pour les ramasser, totalement imperméable à ma présence.

J'épaulai mon arme et la braquai, un geste qu'elle ignora — au point que j'en vins à soupçonner qu'elle n'était rien d'autre qu'un fantôme. Au moment où il me sembla qu'elle me passerait au travers, elle leva les yeux et lâcha ces mots : « L'Herbe est Vivante ».

Je me rendis alors compte à quel point son visage était beau.

Retrouvant mes esprits je répondis : « Naturellement, elle est vivante. »

« nOn », dit-elle, « L'HerBe est VivaNte. »

Je compris ce qu'elle voulait dire. C'était comme si cette herbe étrange se tortillait sans bouger pour autant. Tel un tire-bouchon sur son axe pervers, elle ondulait, s'appropriant perpétuellement le même espace.

« Ce n'est pas réel », affirmai-je, faisant allusion à la situation générale.

« Tout est réel », répondit-elle succinctement.

À cet instant jaillit des ténèbres la source de ces horribles bruits — une salve de tirs tremblants m'échappa. L'écume aux lèvres, trois bêtes vinrent prendre place à ses côtés.

« Ne tirez pas », dit-elle calmement — comme si je n'avais pas la moindre chance d'atteindre quoi que ce soit. « Ils sont à moi, n'ayez aucune crainte. »

Imaginez un peu le contraste émotionnel éprouvé ce jour-là sur le rivage. J'y accostais en grand explorateur, prêt à nommer un royaume inconnu et toute créature qui l'habite. Tout ça pour me découvrir devancé par cette fille frêle et mal vêtue, pour qui les choses allaient plutôt bien selon toute apparence. Et voilà que dans l'instant je tombais amoureux.

Une série de malentendus m'amenèrent à penser qu'elle s'appelait Miss Miss, et elle à croire que mon nom était Only McFew. Miss Miss devait devenir ma camarade et ma marraine sur l'Île — tout en évitant habilement et systématiquement mes avances ultérieures.

Cette nuit-là, je dormis emmitouflé dans mon manteau, allongé sur une vieille chaise longue dans le couloir de son appartement à Onomatopoeia — je n'étais certainement pas le premier homme à pénétrer ici. Plusieurs générations de pélerins, de prospecteurs, de législateurs et de hors-la-loi, d'entrepreneurs, de voyageurs, de missionnaires, de mystiques et de scaldes m'avaient précédé dans ce port.

Je fus réveillé aux aurores par le souffle rance de l'une de ses bêtes sur mon visage. Courbaturé et désorienté, je dus me lever en douceur pour ne pas l'effrayer et entraîner une réaction imprévisible de sa part, avant de me faufiler à travers le couloir jusqu'à la pièce principale.

Son décor était simple et brillant — un sol carrelé d'hexagones noirs, blancs et gris, des murs peints d'un rose vif.
Une grande fenêtre. Quelques unes de ces précieuses herbes trempaient dans un vase posé sur la table. Je fus attiré par ce qui m'apparut être un conteneur placé sur un cube blanc à l'autre bout de la pièce. À l'intérieur s'ébattaient quatre créatures ailées, exécutant une danse selon une symétrie étrange.

En me rapprochant, je vis qu'elles passaient de temps à autre à travers la structure qui avait tout d'abord semblé les retenir. Je tendis la main pour toucher la vitre. Il n'y en avait pas.

« Si elles restent, ce n'est pas par obligation, mais parce que telle est leur volonté », m'expliqua une Miss Miss immaculée qui venait de faire son apparition. « Un peu de thé ? »

Après un petit déjeuner frugal, elle me demanda de partir et de revenir plus tard. Elle attendait la venue d'un imprésario pour ses animaux, auxquels elle avait, semble-t-il, appris à chanter. Elle me suggéra d'aller me promener en ville, et me donna un peu d'argent pour mon déjeuner. Après quoi, me dit-elle, nous devrions retourner à la plage où j'avais laissé mon bateau. Des chercheurs d'algues pourraient le trouver et le détruire, pensant qu'il s'agit de celui d'un concurrent.

Marchant anonymement sur le port, je fus déconcerté par la diversité et l'énergie de l'endroit, me remémorant ma naïveté, moi qui m'étais cru le premier à poser le pied sur ces rivages.

Des touristes par centaines descendaient les passerelles de grands paquebots ballotés contre la jetée. Une foule de colporteurs, de revendeurs, de prostituées et de guides les assaillaient dès leur arrivée à terre.

Il y avait là des cafés, des baraques de fast-food, des femmes portant des sacs provenant de boutiques de luxe ... un essaim d'écolières de passage me lança une obscénité avant de s'éloigner en éclatant de rire.

Plus loin, le rivage témoignait d'une industrie en récession : entrepôts, grandes turbines en déréliction, ainsi qu'un vaste abri coiffé d'une enseigne TRAVAIL. À l'intérieur se trouvaient des établis, deux machines à sous à l'abandon, une urne, et un homme assis à une table, coiffé d'une casquette noire pointue et marquée d'un cercle rouge, qui empilait des tickets.

Au dehors, un groupe d'itinérants prenaient part à une forme d'économie alternative.

Je ne valais pas mieux qu'eux, bien que libéré en un sens par ma faillite. Je n'étais personne, mais n'avais rien à prouver, libre d'explorer cet autre pays qui n'était pas de ma responsabilité, mais tout simplement une chose neuve à appréhender.

C'était également l'occasion de regarder mon futur en face. Le déshonneur d'un retour ne me tentait guère, et ici, sur l'Île, j'étais sous le charme de Miss Miss. Non pas que je semblais l'émouvoir — la probabilité d'être chassé de son couloir était plus grande que celle d'entrer dans sa chambre.

J'étrennai mon nouveau statut de touriste dans la file d'attente de chez *Marcel's Casserole*, pour m'acheter une cocotte de moules et deux œufs.

Je pensais qu'il me fallait l'impressionner, de sorte qu'elle me voit sous un jour différent de celui du vagabond dépenaillé et décontenancé qu'elle avait secouru sur le rivage.

Je persistais à croire que pour m'inviter chez elle avec une telle insouciance, elle devait avoir entrevu chez moi quelque chose qui me différentiait des autres miséreux échoués ici. Était-ce la douceur de mes traits ? D'autres aspects matériels ? Mes bottes couleur vin aux semelles noires ?
Mon aristocratie naturelle ?

L'œuf fut si amer que j'en grimaçai. Mais je persévérai.

Une vieille femme passa en coup de vent, coiffée d'un chapeau noir hérissé qui manqua de m'arracher un œil. On aurait dit un oursin géant posé sur sa tête. Elle semblait de mauvaise humeur. Sur ses talons, un homme en costume s'adressait à elle par des « Maman » et cherchait à la raisonner.

Dans la foule, deux hommes se tenant face à la Penrose Trading Company aiguisèrent mon attention. Ils semblaient différents des hordes d'excursionnistes — raison pour laquelle je décidai de les suivre.

Ils étaient chaudement habillés, vêtus de pulls épais et de manteaux d'hiver, avec des bottes de cuir fin aux pieds. Tout leur équipement était rassemblé dans un chariot : armes, cages, de grandes quantités de cordes neuves, des bidons d'eau ainsi que des bottes en cuir de rechange.

Je ne pus rien distinguer de leur conversation, mais ils s'entretenaient au sujet d'une carte — non pas un banal plan de ville sur lequel figurent les lieux qui importent, mais une grande feuille dépliée recouverte de tracés, de points et de symboles mystérieux, qu'ils manipulaient à grand peine dans le vent.

Je mordis dans mon deuxième œuf.

ÉPILOGUE

Voici la plaine où Rocco trouva un monstre mort.

Sa finesse m'égare profondément.

D'innombrables fleurs blanches s'évanouissent en un halo lumineux infini sur l'horizon — hormis le vent, rien ou presque pour venir ébouriffer la prairie.

Aux limites de mon champ de vision, je crois souvent apercevoir un petit animal qui gambade. L'une de ces observations est-elle pertinente, je ne saurais le dire.

Je baisse le regard pour fouiller le sol, en quête du moindre signe de diversité. Un petit galet ... les ossements d'une créature ... peut-être ... d'étranges lignes serpentines dans la poussière ... une substance mousseuse sur une tige ... une autre pierre ... une vieille bouteille en plastique ! Retournée et secouée, elle déverse un liquide trouble qui disparaît dans le sol.

Nombreux sont ceux à s'être risqués dans la partie la plus retirée de cette île lointaine. Certains en sont revenus pour conter leur histoire. Ceux qui s'affirment en quête de nouveauté rapportent qu'une bête appelée Noumenon vit dans cette atmosphère réifiée, et bien que son existence n'ait jamais été attestée, la conviction qu'elle habite la partie sauvage est profonde. Le reste de l'Île est bien cartographié.

Certains viennent seuls pour ne pas inquiéter la créature, avec l'espoir de l'enchanter. Le témoignage de tels solitaires est cependant écarté comme l'hallucination de l'utopiste ou l'élucubration du charlatan. D'autres viennent accompagnés pour que leurs dires puissent être corroborés. Pas un seul n'a triomphé. « Trois, c'est déjà foule », doit penser Noumenon.

De plus vastes tentatives les réunirent par centaines, équipés de chiens, de filets et de tous les engins imaginables. Ils cherchèrent à encercler la créature sans y parvenir. Noumenon est sans aucun doute un être d'une finesse infinie. Seule la foi fonde son existence, ou comme l'affirme le bon sens : « Il est derrière vous ! »

Un océan d'amnésie existe néanmoins, que les nouvelles générations doivent traverser pour rejoindre l'île. Dotée de l'équipement le plus récent, chaque expédition accoste le rivage et savoure l'air humide — vision de jeunes gens sur la plage, gais et optimistes tandis qu'ils s'avancent vers les ténèbres.

J'ai moi-même été conduit jusqu'ici par le parfum de ce chat énigmatique, à mon grand regret. Je me contenterais volontiers de l'odeur de ses excréments si cela pouvait me délivrer de la situation dans laquelle je me trouve à présent.

Ma faiblesse de caractère me révulse, car je dois bien m'avouer gagné par une solitude écœurante, plus rapidement et plus profondément que je ne l'aurais imaginé. J'aspire à retrouver la solitude de ce café à la lisière d'Onomatopy, d'où est partie cette expédition inconsidérée. Là où un garçon mal poli me servit un café en grande partie renversé dans la soucoupe tandis qu'il badinait avec les barmans et formulait des obscénités sur les femmes qui passaient derrière la vitre, aussi inaccessibles à sa grossièreté qu'à ma timidité. Là où deux gaillards coiffés de hauts-de-forme vinrent s'asseoir près d'un miroir accroché au mur, absorbés par leur conversation.

Un mendiant entra et me marmonna quelque chose en dialecte, à propos de lait pour son bébé (absent) — j'en déduisis qu'il désirait un peu d'argent. Il resta planté devant moi plusieurs secondes après mon refus, m'infligeant de respirer sa puanteur. Bon sang, pensai-je, pourquoi les serveurs ne font-ils rien pour chasser d'ici ce fou ? À mon grand regret, il s'installa alors au bar, apparemment en excellents termes avec le personnel. Il commanda un café impeccablement servi, semble-t-il sur le compte de la maison, avant d'échanger des salutations amicales avec les deux géants assis dans l'angle.

Mais me voici loin d'Onomatopy, et je ne sais comment rentrer. La mort est en réalité plus proche que la ville.

J'ai aperçu hier au loin ce lièvre prétentieux. Il s'arrêta un instant et me lança ce qui m'apparut être un regard apitoyé. J'espérai qu'il m'indiquerait le chemin du retour, mais il se contenta de me montrer ses bagues et passa son chemin. Je glissai après coup deux cartouches dans mon fusil, mais le lièvre s'en était allé depuis longtemps.

Un autre chasseur me raconta un jour que dans cette contrée, la valeur d'un homme se mesure à son arme et à ce que renferment son sac et sa personne. Se remémorer ce que l'on est nécessite de la concentration. Aussi ai-je commencé à écrire. Pour m'aider à me rappeler. Penser, simplement penser n'est pas suffisant : il faut penser : « Je pense ! »

Chaque jour — événement imperceptible sous ces latitudes — je fais le point. Pour rassembler mes esprits, ou plutôt pour me détacher des choses :

Moi : Je me fais appeler Only McFew (si, je vous assure!). Une fille que j'appelle Miss Miss est ma meilleure amie. Bien qu'elle n'en sache rien ou prétende ne rien en savoir, je l'aime. Je suis un homme.

Mon sac : deux crayons. Un cahier. Un bocal. Un couteau, naturellement, pour écorcher ce maudit lièvre le jour où il sera trop audacieux. Un demi paquet de bananes séchées. Un serpent manchot, qui ira rejoindre celui que je garde chez moi si jamais j'y retourne. Montés sur des branches de bois, j'en ferai des presse-livres — une pensée qui me réconforte. Une perforatrice, objet cher à Miss Miss. C'est elle qui me la prêta, il y a un moment de ça. Objet encombrant et totalement inutile, vu les circonstances. Je ne l'ai emporté que pour l'avoir oublié dans mon sac avant de partir. Avec mon attitude débonnaire au début de l'expédition, je n'ai porté aucune attention à son poids.

Mes pensées tournent à la méditation érotique sur Miss Miss.

Je dois être loin au-dessus du monde, je le sais, car voici que les fleurs sont vives sur fond de ciel gris et que j'entends des bruits venus de nulle part, de petites explosions musicales dans l'air, un phénomène qu'il faut percevoir pour le croire, comme ces poissons volants dont j'ai entendu certains marins parler, et dont je ne crois rien.

Tout se passe comme si je marchais latéralement le long du temps, avec mon passé à ma gauche et mon futur à ma droite. Je ne peux continuer de la sorte. Il me faut choisir — un choix que je ne ferai pas, de crainte de faire le mauvais. Aussi, je mets un pied devant l'autre et je continue, avec l'espoir de trouver un signe pour me guider.

Pire que tout, je commence à douter. Je doute sérieusement du Noumenon, me demandant si je n'ai pas offert mes os en sacrifice à la poussière anonyme de la plaine et mis ma vie en péril pour une chimère. (Une fois mort sans résurrection possible, j'imagine que le lièvre s'approchera délicatement de mon corps, que mon anneau grenat ira enrichir sa collection lorsque la chair de mes doigts sera pourrie.)

Je doute de l'affection que me porte Miss Miss. Son moi fataliste peut-il entrevoir dans ma disparition autre chose que le cours des événements ?

Mes inquiétudes ne s'arrêtent pas là. Parfois les fleurs ne sont pas alignées avec leurs tiges. Pourquoi n'ai-je jamais vu le pied d'une montagne ? Apprendre plus que quelques mots d'If'enish m'est impossible, en dépit de ma patience et de mes efforts pour l'étudier — voici que je soupçonne dans cet argot un charabia improvisé pour les touristes.

Et finalement, derrière les boutiques, les bars et les lumières d'Onomatopy, derrière le Plan des Dieux, là où reposent les machines abandonnées et les ordures, sous les montagnes, sous les fleurs, sous la poussière et les ossements des chasseurs, existe-t-il seulement une île ?

Ce texte a été initialement commandé en 2009 à l'occasion de la quatrième parution de « To Hell with Journals » édité par Charles Arsène-Henry et Hans Ulrich Obrist.

ADDENDA

Cet ouvrage a été réalisé à l'occasion de l'exposition *Onomatopoeia : part 1* de Charles Avery, présentée au Plateau / Frac Île-de-France à Paris, au Kunstverein de Hanovre et au EX3 à Florence.

Charles Avery se consacre depuis 2005 à une œuvre épique portant sur une île imaginaire, œuvre qui mêle dessins, objets, installations et textes.
L'île, qui n'a pas de nom particulier, figure au centre d'un archipel en forme de spirale, composé d'innombrables îlots bordés d'un océan noir. Nos connaissances sur cette *terra incognita* proviennent du témoignage d'un jeune homme – dont on n'apprendra jamais le nom – qui, échoué sur un rivage isolé de l'île, croit en être le découvreur avant de déchanter et d'être ramené à la raison par une jeune femme qu'il rencontre sur le rivage.

The Islanders peut être entendu de différentes manières : une méditation portant sur les thèmes centraux de la philosophie, une critique de toutes les grandes dualités – conscient et inconscient, réel et irréel, le 1 et le 2 – ou bien une métaphore de l'emprise d'une vision coloniale sur le monde des idées.

La première exposition majeure du projet, intitulée simplement *The Islanders : an introduction*, s'est tenue en 2008 à Parasol unit, Londres, avant d'être successivement accueillie par la Gallery of Modern Art d'Edimbourg et par le Musée Boijmans van Beuningen de Rotterdam. Cette exposition et l'ouvrage qui l'accompagnait cherchaient à décrire les caractéristiques les plus saillantes de l'Île, en offrant un aperçu du projet comme *work in progress* tout en faisant état de son ambition et de son envergure à venir. Depuis lors, le projet s'est focalisé sur une exploration détaillée de la ville d'Onomatopoeia, la seule cité que compte l'Île, un ancien avant-poste colonial devenu successivement une ville champignon et une place commerciale florissante, puis un bidonville frappé par la récession, régénéré en destination touristique.

Les expositions au Plateau / Frac Île-de-France à Paris, au Kunstverein de Hanovre ainsi qu'à EX3 à Florence sont les premières présentations majeures de cette phase importante du projet. Elles constituent également les premières expositions personnelles de l'œuvre de l'artiste en France, en Allemagne et en Italie.

Cet ouvrage est consacré à un seul et unique dessin de grandes dimensions (plus de 5 m sur 2 m 40) représentant le port d'Onomatopoeia. Point d'arrivée et de départ de cet espace fictionnel, il constitue le centre de la ville et de l'Île, et il résume parfaitement le projet dans sa totalité.

Les directeurs des différentes institutions tiennent à remercier Charles Avery pour l'engagement exceptionnel qui fut le sien pour la mise en œuvre des expositions successives ainsi que pour la réalisation de cet ouvrage. Ils remercient également Marc Kappeler pour la conception graphique du catalogue, ainsi que les galeries doggerfisher (Edinburgh), Pilar Corrias (Londres) et Sonia Rosso (Turin) pour leur aide logistique et financière.

Pour le soutien apporté aux différentes expositions du projet, Le Plateau / Frac Île-de-France remercie le Conseil régional d'Île-de-France, le Ministère de la culture et de la communication et la Ville de Paris. Le Kunstverein de Hanovre remercie le Ministère de la Science et de la Culture de Basse-Saxe, la banque NORD / LB et la Stiftung Horizonte. EX3 remercie la Commune de Florence et le projet Toscanaincontemporanea de la Région Toscane.

Xavier Franceschi
Directeur, Le Plateau / Frac Île-de-France, Paris

René Zechlin
Directeur, Kunstverein, Hanovre

Sergio Tossi
Directeur, EX3, Florence

PROLOG

Die Insel betrat ich zum ersten Mal gegen Ende des großen Seetang-Rauschs, von dem ich damals noch nichts wusste. Ich war auf der Suche nach diesem Land gewesen, in der Hoffnung, sein Entdecker zu werden.

Mit letzter Kraft und gezeichnet von dem Kampf gegen die Gezeiten und den Regen und das unendliche Gestrüpp aus Seetang, das sich um meine Paddel gewunden hatte, zog ich mein Boot an Land.

Ich warf meine Tasche auf die Erde, lehnte mein Gewehr gegen einen großen Stein und schälte eine Banane.

Es war dunkel, dicke Regentropfen klatschten mir ins Gesicht. Ich konnte nichts sehen, also lauschte ich. Ich vernahm das Knistern des Blasentangs im Wind, ich hörte, wie der Regen auf den Lehmboden platschte, und das Knacksen und die Rufe unbekannter Tiere, die in Abgeschiedenheit lebten.

Als ich mir eine zweite Banane schmecken ließ, fing ich an, mich in Gedanken über den Empfang, der mich bei meiner Rückkehr nach Triangland erwarten würde, zu verlieren: die Fahnenschwenker auf dem Pier, ein Interview mit dem *Fancy That* Magazin, eine Grußbotschaft von der Regierung.

Während ich das Gefühl vollkommener Erfüllung genoss, bemerkte ich aus dem Augenwinkel, wie sich etwas bewegte. Ich drehte den Kopf und sah eine Steinmaus, die sich im Gestein zu tarnen versuchte: halb Tier, halb Mineral, deren Herz nur alle tausend Jahre schlägt und für die selbst die kleinste Bewegung mit äußersten Qualen verbunden ist. Ich würde dieses neuartige Wesen zurück in die Heimat mitnehmen und es dem Premier als Souvenir dieser erstaunlichen neuen Welt überreichen. Ich nahm ein altes Einmachglas aus meiner Tasche und schaffte die Kreatur samt eines Teils seiner feuchten Umgebung hinein. Es regnete nun stärker, und grauenhafte kleine Geräusche, die scheinbar näherkamen, drangen aus der Dunkelheit. Ich versuchte, sie zu ignorieren.

Doch als ich den Deckel zuschraubte, erschreckte mich ein anderes, vertrauteres Geräusch: ein menschliches.

Als ich den Blick landeinwärts wendete, sah ich eine blasse Figur, die mir entgegenkam: Eine junge Frau, wie es sich herausstellte, die mit einem Korb in der Hand von Stein zu Stein hüpfte und, wie es schien, mit sich selbst sprach. Sie trug ein durchnässtes und am Saum verschlammtes Unterkleid, eine dünne Strickjacke und Gummistiefel. Sie war offensichtlich erpicht auf irgendein Kraut, das sie, immer wieder innehaltend, von den Steinen sammelte. Mich bemerkte sie gar nicht.

Ich nahm mein Gewehr von der Schulter und brachte es in Anschlag – eine Bewegung, die sie ignorierte. Also vermutete ich, sie sei lediglich ein Geist. In dem Moment, als ich dachte, sie würde glatt durch mich hindurchgehen, blickte sie auf und sagte: »Das Gras ist lebendig.«

Ihr Gesicht war, wie ich nun bemerkte, wunderschön.

Ich sammelte mich und erwiderte: »Natürlich ist es lebendig.«

»NeIN«, sagte sie, »das GraS ist LeBendig.«

Ich wusste, worauf sie hinauswollte, denn dieses merkwürdige Kraut schien sich zu winden, obwohl es sich nicht bewegte. Es nahm weiterhin denselben Raum ein, drehte sich aber wie ein Korkenzieher um seine eigene verkehrte Achse.

»Das ist nicht wirklich,« behauptete ich in Anspielung auf die Situation im Allgemeinen.

»Alles ist wirklich,« lautete ihre knappe Erwiderung.

In diesem Moment sprangen die Verursacher der grauenhaften kleinen Geräusche aus der Dunkelheit – zitternd gab ich einen Schuss ab. Drei geifernde Tiere gesellten sich an ihre Seite.

»Nicht schießen,« sagte sie mit ruhiger Stimme, als hätte ich nicht die geringste Chance, irgendetwas zu treffen. »Sie gehören zu mir. Hab keine Angst.«

Man stelle sich die widersprüchlichen Gefühlszustände vor, die ich damals am Strand durchlebte. Ich war dort an Land gegangen im Glauben, ich sei ein bedeutender Entdecker, der Namensgeber eines neuen Territoriums und von allem, was sich darauf befindet – nur um dann zu erfahren, dass dieses schmächtige, unzureichend gekleidete und offensichtlich äußerst erfolgreiche Mädchen mir zuvorgekommen war Gleichzeitig verliebte ich mich in sie.

Durch eine Folge von Missverständnissen glaubte ich, ihr Name sei Miss Miss und sie, meiner sei Only McFew. Auf der Insel wurde Miss Miss meine Begleiterin und Fürsprecherin – dabei ging sie meinen weiteren Annäherungsversuchen konsequent und geschickt aus dem Wege.

In jener Nacht schlief ich unter meinem Mantel auf einer alten Chaiselongue im Flur ihrer Wohnung, in dem Städtchen Onomatopoeia – denn es stellte sich heraus, dass ich nicht der erste Mensch war, der die Insel betreten hatte; vor mir hatte es Generationen von Pilgern, Prospektoren und Suchenden, von Gesetzesmachern und Gesetzesbrechern, Unternehmern, Wanderarbeitern, Missionaren, Mystikern und Barden gegeben, die alle hier in diesem Hafen gelandet waren.

Früh wurde ich durch den ranzigen Atem eines ihrer Haustiere, das auf meinem Gesicht saß, geweckt. Steif und orientierungslos, erhob ich mich vorsichtig, um das Tier nicht zu alarmieren und eine unvorhersehbare Reaktion zu provozieren. Ich trottete durch den Flur in den großen Raum.

Dieser war schlicht und gleichzeitig lebhaft eingerichtet. Der Fußboden war abwechselnd mit schwarzen, grauen und weißen Sechsecken gefliest, und die Wände waren grell Rosa gestrichen. Es gab einen Tisch, auf dem eine Vase mit dem wertvollen Gras stand, und ein großes Fenster. Am anderen Ende des Raums zog mich ein anderer Einrichtungsgegenstand an. Auf einem weißen Quader an der Wand stand eine Art Tank, in dem vier geflügelte Dinge umeinander herumflatterten. Ihr Tanz hatte etwas merkwürdig Symmetrisches an sich, und als ich mich näherte, sah ich, dass sie gelegentlich aus dem Gebilde, in das sie zunächst eingefasst schienen, ausbrachen. Ich streckte meine Hand aus, um das Glas zu berühren, doch da war nichts.

»Sie bleiben nicht dort, weil sie müssen, sondern weil es ihnen gefällt,« erklärte Miss Miss, die tadellos gekleidet aufgetaucht war. »Tee?«

Nach einem bescheidenen Frühstück bat mich Miss Miss, zu gehen und später wiederzukommen, da sie einen Impressario erwartete, der ihre Tiere, denen sie offensichtlich das Singen beigebracht hatte, begutachten wollte. Sie schlug mir vor, durch das Städtchen zu spazieren, und gab mir etwas Geld für ein Mittagsmahl. Sie sagte, ich sollte anschließend zum Strand, an dem ich mein Boot zurückgelassen hatte, zurückkehren, da Seetangsucher es finden und, wenn sie der Meinung wären, es gehörte einem Konkurrenten, zerstören könnten.

Fremd und anonym lief ich durch den Hafen und war von der Energie und der Vielfalt dieses Orts verblüfft. Ich wunderte mich über meine Naivität, geglaubt zu haben, ich wäre der erste Mensch gewesen, der diese Küste betreten hätte.

Hunderte Touristen strömten entlang der Landungsstege von den großen Passagierschiffen am Pier. Sobald sie von Bord gingen, wurden sie von Scharen von Hausierern, Dealern, Prostituierten und Fremdenführern umzingelt.

Es gab Cafés, Schnellimbisse, Frauen mit Einkaufstüten aus teueren Boutiquen ... eine Schar von Schulmädchen auf Ausflug lief vorbei, einige sagten etwas Anzügliches zu mir und lachten sich kaputt, als sie weitergingen.

Weiter an der Küste entlang gab es Anzeichen von Industrie – und von Rezession: Lagerhäuser, große stillgelegte Turbinen, eine große Unterkunft mit einem Schild auf dem Dach, worauf ARBEIT stand. Im Innern waren lange Bänke, einige kaputte Spielautomaten, ein Kessel und ein Mann, der eine schwarze spitze Mütze mit einem roten Kreis vorne trug und an einem Tisch Tickets sortierte.

Draußen beschäftigte sich eine Gruppe von Wanderarbeitern mit irgendeiner alternativen Ökonomie.

Nun war ich nicht anders als sie, doch irgendwie gab mir mein Bankrott ein Gefühl der Befreiung: Ich war ein Niemand, der nichts beweisen musste; frei, dieses andere Land zu erkunden, das nicht mehr in meiner Verantwortung lag, sondern schlicht etwas Neues war, etwas, das wahrgenommen werden konnte. Es bot mir auch die Gelegenheit, über meine Zukunft nachzudenken, denn mir war nicht nach einer schmachvollen Heimkehr, und hier auf der Insel gab es die Anziehungskraft von Miss Miss – nicht, dass sie von mir gerührt schien, und so, wie ich die Dinge sah, war es wahrscheinlicher, dass sie mich aus ihrem Flur verbannen, als dass sie mich in ihr Schlafzimmer lassen würde.

Ich kam meinem neuen Status als Tourist nach, indem ich in einer Schlange stand, um bei *Marcel's Casserole* eine Tüte Muscheln und zwei Eier zu kaufen.

Ich dachte, dass ich sie beeindrucken musste, damit sie mich in einem anderen Licht sehen würde, nicht in dem des heruntergekommenen und verwirrten Streuners, den sie am Strand gerettet hatte.

Dennoch glaubte ich, dass sie etwas an mir bemerkt haben musste, das mich von den vielen anderen Mittellosen, die hierhergekommen waren, unterschied. Sonst hätte sie mich nicht so unbekümmert zu sich nach Hause eingeladen. War es mein sanfter Teint? Meine Weltferne? Die weinroten Gummistiefel mit schwarzen Sohlen? Die naturgegebene aristokratische Haltung?

Das Ei war so widerlich bitter, dass ich zusammenzuckte, doch ich aß es trotzdem.

Eine alte Frau fegte vorbei, mit einem stacheligen Hut, der mir fast das Auge ausstach. Er sah aus wie ein riesiger Seeigel auf ihrem Kopf. Sie lief schnell und schien verärgert. Dicht an ihren Fersen lief ein Mann in einem Anzug, der auf sie einredete und sie »Mutter« nannte.

In der Menge vor der Penrose Trading Company sah ich zwei Herren stehen, die mich interessierten, denn sie waren, wie es schien, dabei, etwas anderes zu tun als die Horden derTagesausflügler. Also hielt ich mich hinter ihnen.

Sie trugen dicke Pullover, große Mäntel und feine Lederstiefel. Und sie hatten einen Handwagen voller Ausrüstungsgegenstände: Gewehre, Käfige, große Mengen makelloser Seile, Wasserbehälter und zusätzliche Lederstiefel.

Ich konnte ihr Gespräch nicht verstehen, doch sie berieten sich über einer Landkarte – es war kein normaler Stadtplan mit eingezeichneten Sehenswürdigkeiten, sondern ein großes, auseinandergefaltetes Blatt, das zu handhaben ihnen im Wind Schwierigkeiten bereitete, übersät mit obskuren Konturen, Punkten und Symbolen.

Ich nahm einen Bissen von meinem zweiten Ei.

EPILOG

Das ist die Ebene, in der Rocco einst ein totes Monster fand.

In ihrer Spärlichkeit fühle ich mich vollkommen verloren.

Unmengen runder weißer Blumen verschwinden im endlosen Lichtring am Horizont, und abgesehen vom Wind gibt es wenig, was die Weiden in Bewegung setzt.

Hin und wieder glaube ich, am Rande meines Gesichtsfelds ein kleines Tier vorbeihuschen zu sehen, doch sind diese Wahrnehmungen nicht eindeutig.

Ich beschließe, nach unten zu schauen und den Boden nach möglichen Anzeichen von Vielfalt abzusuchen. Ein kleiner flacher Stein ... die Überreste einer kleinen und längst toten Kreatur ... womöglich ... merkwürdige S-förmige Linien im Staub ... irgendeine schaumige Substanz auf einem Stiel ... ein weiterer Stein ... eine alte Plastikflasche! Wenn man sie umkippt und schüttelt, tropft eine trübe Flüssigkeit heraus und versickert in der Erde.

Viele haben sich in diese abgelegene Gegend der weit entfernten Insel begeben. Einige kehren wieder, um ihre Geschichte zu erzählen. Diejenigen, die wiederkehren, sagen, sie seien auf der Suche nach etwas Neuem hergereist, denn in der Vorstellung des Jägers könnte eine Bestie namens Noumenon in dieser reifizierten Atmosphäre hausen. Die Existenz dieser Kreatur ist nie nachgewiesen worden, doch es herrscht die tiefe Überzeugung, dass sie in dieser Wildnis existiert; der Rest der Insel ist nämlich bestens kartographisiert.

Einige kommen alleine, um die Kreatur nicht zu verschrecken und in der Hoffnung, sie zu verzaubern – doch alle Sichtungen, von denen diese Einzelgänger berichten, werden als durch die Höhe verursachte Halluzinationen des Wunschdenkens oder als Lügenmärchen von Scharlatanen abgetan. Andere kommen zu zweit, damit es eine Person gibt, die die Sichtung bezeugen kann, doch diese Paare hatten nie Erfolg. Es scheint, als seien drei Leute schon zuviel, wenn es um das Noumenon geht.

Dann gab es groß angelegte Unterfangen, bei denen hunderte Menschen hierherkamen, mit Hunden und Netzen und allen möglichen Apparaturen ausgerüstet, um die Kreatur zu umzingeln – ohne Erfolg. Es handelt sich eindeutig um ein Wesen mit unendlicher Finesse. Seine Existenz wird nur durch Glauben aufrecht erhalten oder, wie es in einem Kommentar von The Urbane Wit hieß: Es liegt hinter dir!

Nichtsdestotrotz gibt es ein Meer von Amnesie, das neue Generationen überqueren müssen, um diese Insel zu erreichen. Und wenn sie ihre Barken an Land ziehen und die feuchte Luft riechen – jede Expedition mit der jeweils neusten Ausrüstung –, bietet sich einem das Bild fröhlicher junger Frauen und Männer am Strand, die sich voller Optimismus auf den Weg in die Dunkelheit begeben.

Auch ich wurde hierhergelockt durch den Geruch dieser rätselhaften Katze, und ich bedauere es sehr. Ich würde mich mit dem Anblick ihres Kots zufrieden geben, würde ich aus der Situation, in der ich mich jetzt befinde, erlöst werden.

Mir ist meine Charakterschwäche zuwider, denn ich muss zugeben, dass ich von einer unerträglichen Einsamkeit gepackt worden bin, schneller und tiefer gehend, als ich es mir je hätte vorstellen können. Ich sehne mich danach, in die zwar nur unwesentlich weniger einsame Situation des Cafés im Außenposten von Onomatopy zurückverpflanzt zu werden, dort, wo ich diese törichte Expedition plante; wo ein unfreundlicher Kellner mir den Kaffee hinknallte und der größte Teil desselben in der Untertasse landete; der sich nur mit dem Barkeeper scherzhaft unterhielt und anzügliche Kommentare zu den unnahbaren Frauen abgab (in seinem Fall waren sie unnahbar wegen seiner Grobheit, in meinem wegen meiner Schüchternheit), die am Fenster vorbeischlenderten; wo zwei riesige Männer mit Zylindern auffielen, die im Gespräch vertieft neben einem Spiegel an der Wand saßen.

Ein Bettler betrat das Café und nuschelte mich in einem Dialekt an – es ging um Milch für sein (nicht anwesendes) Baby – und ich nahm an, er wollte Kleingeld von mir. Ich winkte ab, doch er blieb noch kurz in meiner Nähe, und ich musste seinen Gestank ertragen. Verdammt, dachte ich, warum schreiten die Kellner nicht ein und entfernen diesen Blödmann. Zu meinem Unbehagen nahm er dann Platz an der Bar, wo er sich offensichtlich gut mit dem Personal verstand. Er trank einen Kaffee, der ihm einwandfrei und, wie es schien, aufs Haus, serviert wurde. Dabei grüßte er die beiden Riesen in der Ecke freundlich.

Nun bin ich allerdings weit von Onomatopy entfernt, und der Weg zurück ist mir unbekannt. Tatsächlich ist der Tod näher als dieses Städtchen.

Gestern sah ich diesen Angeber-Hasen von Weitem. Er hielt kurz inne – und blickte in meine Richtung, so dachte ich zumindest, voller Selbstmitleid. Ich hoffte, er würde mir den Weg nach Hause weisen. Stattdessen ließ er seine Ringe in meine Richtung blitzen und eilte weiter. Daraufhin fummelte ich ein paar Patronen in mein Gewehr, doch da war der Hase längst weg.

Ein anderer Jäger erzählte mir, dass alles, was du hier draußen wirklich bist, sich aus dem Inhalt deiner Tasche, deines Ichs und deinem Gewehr zusammensetzt. Du musst dich konzentrieren, um dich an das zu erinnern, was du bist. Deswegen habe ich angefangen, zu schreiben, damit ich mich besser erinnern kann. Es reicht nicht zu denken, du musst denken: »Jetzt denke ich!«

Jeden Tag – und das ist ein fein ausgedachtes Ereignis in diesen Breiten – mache ich Inventur, um mich zusammenzuhalten, oder besser gesagt, um die Dinge auf Distanz zu halten:

Ich: Ich heiße Only McFew (ehrlich!). Mein bester Freund ist ein Mädchen – ich nenne sie Miss Miss. Ich bin in sie verliebt, doch davon ahnt sie nichts, zumindest tut sie so, als merkte sie nichts. Ich bin ein Mann.

Tasche: Zwei Bleistifte. Ein Notizheft. Ein Einmachglas. Ein Messer, natürlich um diesen verdammten Hasen zu häuten, wenn er denn zu frech wird. Eine halbe Tüte getrockneter Bananenscheiben. Eine einarmige Schlange. Ich werde sie neben der anderen, die ich zu Hause habe, platzieren, wenn ich es jemals dorthin zurückschaffe. Ich werde sie auf L-förmigen Holzstücken anbringen und als Buchstützen benutzen. Das ist ein aufmunternder Gedanke. Ein Locher, den mir Miss Miss vor einiger Zeit ausgeliehen hat und an dem ich sehr hänge (er ist allerdings ein belastender Ausrüstungsgegenstand und unter den gegenwärtigen Umständen absolut nutzlos.) Ich trage ihn bei mir, weil ich vergessen habe, ihn aus der Tasche zu nehmen, bevor ich loszog; wie schwer er ist, ist mir wegen meiner Unbeschwertheit zu Beginn der Expedition überhaupt nicht aufgefallen.

Meine Gedanken wandern zu erotischen Betrachtungen über Miss Miss.

Ich bin mir sicher, dass ich mich auf einem erhöhten Punkt der Erde befinde, denn die Blumen leuchten kräftig gegen den dunkelgrauen Himmel, und ich höre Geräusche ohne Quelle, kleine musikalische Explosionen in der Luft – ein Phänomen, das man gehört haben muss, um es zu glauben: wie fliegende Fische, von denen ich Seeleute habe sprechen hören (und denen ich keinen Glauben schenke).

Mir kommt es vor, als laufe ich seitwärts durch die Zeit, meine Vergangenheit zur Linken, meine Zukunft zur Rechten. Ich kann so nicht weitermachen. Ich muss eine Wahl treffen, doch nicht aus Furcht, es könnte die falsche sein. Ich mache einfach weiter, setze einen Fuß vor den anderen und hoffe auf ein Zeichen, das mir den Weg zeigt.

Inzwischen – und das ist das Schlimmste – fange ich an zu zweifeln. Ich bezweifele ernsthaft das Noumenon, und frage mich, ob ich mein Leben aufs Spiel gesetzt und meine Knochen dem namenlosen Staub der Ebene geopfert habe nur wegen einer Chimäre. (Ich stelle mir vor, wie der Hase sich zaghaft meiner Leiche nähert, sobald er sicher ist, dass ich jenseits der Möglichkeit einer Wiederauferstehung tot bin, und wenn das Fleisch an meinen Fingern verfault ist, wird er sich meinen Granatring für seine Sammlung krallen.)

Ich hege Zweifel an der Zuneigung von Miss Miss. Wird ihr fatalistisches Ego meinen Tod anders als den Lauf der Dinge betrachten?

Auch Anderes irritiert mich inzwischen: Zuweilen stehen die Blumenblüten nicht ganz in einer Linie mit ihren Stielen. Warum habe ich niemals den Fuß eines Berges gesehen? Obwohl ich mir Mühe gegeben habe, die If'enische Sprache zu erlernen, habe ich mir nur wenige Worte aneignen können – ich glaube deshalb, dass dieser Argot lediglich ein improvisiertes Kauderwelsch für die Ohren der Touristen ist.

Und schließlich frage ich mich, ob – jenseits der Geschäfte und Bars und Lichter von Onomatopy, jenseits der Ebene der Götter, wo ausrangierte Maschinen und Müll verstreut liegen, unter den Bergen und den Blumen und dem Staub und den Knochen der Jäger – eine Insel überhaupt existiert?

Dieser Text wurde erstmals abgedruckt in der vierten Ausgabe von *To Hell with Journals*, herausgegeben von Charles Arsène-Henry und Hans Ulrich Obrist, 2009.

ADDENDA

Das vorliegende Buch wurde anlässlich der Ausstellung Charles Avery – *Onomatopoeia: part 1* im Le Plateau / Frac Île-de-France, Paris, im Kunstverein Hannover und im EX3, Florenz produziert.

Seit 2005 arbeitet Charles Avery an einer episch angelegten Werkgruppe, die mit Zeichnungen, Objekten, Installationen und Texten eine fiktionale Insel heraufbeschwört. Die Insel, die einfach »Island« heißt, befindet sich im Mittelpunkt eines spiralförmigen Archipels unzähliger kleinerer Inseln umgeben von tiefschwarzem Meer. Die Kenntnisse dieser *Terra incognita* verdanken wir den Berichten eines jungen Mannes – dessen Namen wir ebenfalls nie erfahren –, der an einer abgelegenen Küste der Insel an Land geht und meint, ihr Entdecker zu sein. Doch schon bald erfährt er von einer jungen Frau, die er dort trifft, dass dies ein Irrglaube war. Nun muss er den Sinn und Zweck seines Lebens radikal überdenken.

The Islanders kann auf vielfältige Weise verstanden werden: als ein Nachdenken über die zentralen Themen der Philosophie, als Kritik aller großer Dualismen wie z. B. bewusst und unbewusst, wirklich und unwirklich, 1 und 2 oder als Metapher für die kolonialistisch geprägte Aufteilung und Inbesitznahme der Ideenwelt.

2008 fand bei Parasol unit in London die erste große Ausstellung dieses Projekts unter dem simplen Titel »The Islanders: an introduction« statt, die im Anschluss in der Gallery of Modern Art, Edinburgh, und im Museum Boijmans van Beuningen, Rotterdam, gezeigt wurde. Jene Ausstellung und das begleitende Buch markierten den Versuch, die wichtigsten Eigenschaften der Insel zu beschreiben und Einblicke in das Projekt zu geben – als »Work in Progress« und als ein Statement zu den künftigen Zielen und dem Umfang des Unterfangens. Seitdem konzentriert sich das Projekt auf eine detaillierte Erkundung der einzigen Stadt der Insel namens Onomatopoeia: einst ein kolonialer Außenposten, daraufhin »Boomtown«, dann ein florierendes Handelszentrum, dann ein von der Rezession geplagter Slum und schließlich ein wiedererblühtes touristisches Ausflugsziel.

Die Ausstellungen im Le Plateau / Frac Île-de-France, Paris, dem Kunstverein Hannover und EX3, Florenz, sind die ersten großen Präsentationen dieser wichtigen Phase des Projekts und zugleich die ersten institutionellen Einzelausstellungen des Künstlers in Frankreich, Deutschland und Italien.

Dieses Buch widmet sich einer einzigen, großformatigen Zeichnung (2,4 x 5 m) des Hafens von Onomatopoeia. Als Ankunfts- und Abfahrtsort dieser fiktionalen Inselwelt, als Mittelpunkt der Stadt und der Insel, stellt er eine ideale Verdichtung des gesamten Projekts dar.

Die Direktoren der Institutionen danken Charles Avery für sein außergewöhnliches Engagement für die Ausstellungen und die Publikation, Marc Kappeler für die grafische Gestaltung des Katalogs sowie den Galerien doggerfisher, Edinburgh, Pilar Corrias, London, und Sonia Rosso, Turin, für ihre organisatorische und finanzielle Unterstützung.

Für die Ermöglichung des Projekts an den verschiedenen Ausstellungsorten dankt Le Plateau / Frac Île-de-France, Paris le Conseil régional d'Île-de-France, le Ministère de la culture et de la communication und la Ville de Paris, der Kunstverein Hannover dem Niedersächsischen Ministerium für Wissenschaft und Kultur, der NORD / LB und der Stiftung Horizonte, und EX3 dankt der Commune di Firenze und dem Projekt Toscanaincontemporanea der Region Toskana.

Xavier Franceschi
Direktor, Le Plateau / Frac Île-de-France, Paris

René Zechlin
Direktor, Kunstverein Hannover

Sergio Tossi
Direktor, EX3, Florenz

PROLOGO

Giunsi per la prima volta sull'isola al termine della grande migrazione Kelp, sebbene all'epoca non lo sapessi. Al contrario, avevo cercato questa terra con l'intento di esserne lo scopritore.

Trascinai la barca sulla spiaggia con le ultime forze che mi erano rimaste dopo aver lottato contro la marea, la pioggia e le foreste di alghe che avevano ricoperto i remi.

Misi giù lo zaino, appoggiai il fucile contro una larga roccia e sbucciai una banana.

Non potendo vedere molto lontano a causa dell'oscurità e della pioggia che m'inondava gli occhi, mi misi in ascolto. Sentii le querce marine crepitare nell'impeto, il cicaleccio della pioggia sulla terra battuta, gli schiocchi e lo stridere di artigli di bestie sconosciute muoversi verso le loro esistenze nascoste.

Non appena ebbi finito di mangiare con gusto una seconda banana, mi misi a fantasticare sull'accoglienza che mi attendeva al mio ritorno a Triangland: le bandiere alzate sui pennoni, un'intervista con *Fancy That*, un messaggio dal governo.

Mentre assaporavo una sensazione di totale appagamento, con la coda dell'occhio scorsi qualcosa che si muoveva. Volsi la testa e vidi un ratto-pietra che cercava di mimetizzarsi in un gruppo di sassi: metà animale, metà minerale, con un cuore che batte una volta ogni migliaio di anni e per il quale il più piccolo movimento rappresenta una contorsione agonizzante. Avrei portato questo nuovo essere a casa per donarlo al Presidente come ricordo di questo incredibile nuovo mondo. Presi dunque un vecchio barattolo di cetrioli dallo zaino e iniziai a sollevare la creatura, assieme ad una parte del terreno umido circostante. La pioggia aveva cominciato a battere forte e dall'oscurità emergevano orrendi rumori di sottofondo, la cui sorgente sembrava avvicinarsi. Cercai di ignorarli.

Non appena strizzai le palpebre tuttavia, sobbalzai per un altro suono, ben più familiare: quello dell'Umanità.

Dando le spalle alla terra, riuscii a scorgere una figura pallida venire verso di me dalla costa: ne emerse una ragazza che, con in mano un cesto, saltava da una roccia all'altra parlando, apparentemente a se stessa. Indossava una sottoveste, fradicia e fangosa lungo l'orlo, un cardigan leggero e stivali di gomma. Sembrava rapita da un qualche genere di erbaccia che a tratti si fermava a cogliere dalle rocce, del tutto indifferente alla mia presenza.

Mi tolsi il fucile di spalla e lo alzai, ma lei m'ignorò del tutto, tanto da farmi sospettare che altro non fosse che un fantasma. Non appena fu tanto vicina da farmi credere che mi sarebbe passata attraverso, alzò gli occhi e disse: "L'Erba Vive".

Il suo volto, ormai chiaro, era bellissimo.

Mi ricomposi e replicai "Certo, è viva."

"nO", disse. "L'ErBa ViVe."

Capii ciò che intendeva; quella strana erbaccia sembrava contorcersi, pur senza spostarsi. Piuttosto, continuava ad occupare lo stesso spazio, avvitandosi come un cavatappi sul proprio asse distorto.

"Tutto ciò non è reale", dissi, alludendo all'intera situazione.

"Ogni cosa è reale", replicò lei, seccamente.

In quel momento, dall'oscurità balzarono fuori le cause di quei terribili rumori di sottofondo – e lasciai partire uno sparo tremolante. Tre belve con le fauci schiumeggianti erano comparse al suo fianco.

"Non sparare", disse con tono calmo, come se io non avessi alcuna speranza di colpire alcunché. "Sono mie. Non avere paura".

Provate ad immaginare il vortice di emozioni che provai quel giorno sulla spiaggia. Ero approdato pensando di essere un esploratore di alto rango, il cui nome avrebbe indicato un nuovo regno e ogni cosa ad esso appartenente, solo per scoprire che ero stato sconfitto da questa esile ragazza mal vestita, che apparentemente aveva vinto. E in tutto ciò, mi ero innamorato.

Attraverso una serie di fraintendimenti, finii col pensare che si chiamasse Miss Miss, e lei che il mio nome fosse Only Mc Few. Miss Miss sarebbe diventata la mia compagna e madrina sull'isola, evitando al contempo fermamente e abilmente ogni mia ulteriore avance.

Quella notte dormii coprendomi col cappotto su una vecchia poltrona a sdraio nel corridoio del suo appartamento, nella città di Onomatopoeia. Si capiva che non ero neanche il primo uomo a mettervi piede, ma che ero stato preceduto da diverse generazioni di pellegrini, cercatori, passanti, uomini di legge e fuorilegge, imprenditori, girovaghi, missionari, mistici e vati, che avevano tutti già varcato questa porta.

Fui svegliato presto dal fiato rancido sulla faccia di uno dei suoi animali da compagnia. Indolenzito e disorientato, mi alzai piano, in modo da non agitare la creatura e provocarne una reazione imprevedibile e mi mossi lentamente verso la stanza principale.

Aveva un aspetto semplice e vivace. Il pavimento era ricoperto da mattonelle nere, grigie e bianche alternate in modo da formare degli esagoni, mentre le pareti erano dipinte di un rosa brillante. C'erano un tavolo su cui spiccava un vaso contenente la preziosa erbaccia e un'ampia finestra. Dal lato più distante della stanza, un altro oggetto attirò la mia attenzione. Su un cubo bianco accanto alla parete si trovava quella che sembrava essere una tanica in cui quattro cose alate svolazzavano l'una contro l'altra. C'era una strana simmetria nel loro danzare e non appena mi fui avvicinato, vidi che ogni tanto trapassavano attraverso la struttura che in un primo momento era sembrata contenerle. Avvicinai la mano al vetro per toccarlo, ma non c'era.

"Non restano lì dentro perché devono, restano lì dentro perché vogliono", mi spiegò Miss Miss, apparsa dal nulla nella stanza. "Del tè?"

Dopo una colazione frugale, Miss Miss mi disse di andarmene e di tornare più tardi, visto che un impresario sarebbe venuto a vedere i suoi animali, ai quali sembrava avesse insegnato a cantare. Mi suggerì di fare due passi in città e mi dette dei soldi per comprarmi il pranzo. Più tardi, disse, saremmo dovuti tornare alla spiaggia su cui avevo lasciato la mia barca, perché se i Kelp l'avessero trovata l'avrebbero certamente distrutta, credendola di un rivale.

Camminando anonimamente lungo il porto fui colpito dall'energia e dalla varietà del posto e mi meravigliai della mia ingenuità nell'aver pensato di essere il primo a metter piede su quelle coste.

Centinaia di turisti si riversavano lungo le passerelle di grandi navi passeggeri che si facevano largo verso il molo; non appena sbarcati, quegli stessi turisti sarebbero stati presi d'assalto da schiere di guide, spacciatori e prostitute.

C'erano caffè, fast food, signore con in mano sacchetti di costose boutique ... un branco di ragazze in gita mi gridò qualcosa di osceno, per poi andarsene ridendo.

In lontananza, lungo la costa, si scorgevano segni d'industrializzazione – e di recessione: magazzini, grandi turbine ormai in disuso, un'ampia tettoia con sopra scritto MANODOPERA. Dentro vi si trovavano alcuni lunghi banchi, un paio di vecchie macchine mangiasoldi, un'urna e un uomo seduto a un tavolo con indosso un cappello nero appuntito e un cerchio rosso sulla fronte, a smistare biglietti.

Fuori, un gruppo di viaggiatori era stato coinvolto in una sorta di economia alternativa.

Contavo né più né meno di loro, eppure mi sentii liberato dalla mia bancarotta: ero un perfetto sconosciuto che non aveva niente da dimostrare, libero di esplorare quest'altro paese di cui non ero più responsabile, ma che mi appariva semplicemente come qualcosa di nuovo da percepire.

Mi si offriva anche un'opportunità di contemplare il mio futuro: non immaginavo infatti con piacere un ritorno vergognoso in patria, mentre lì sull'isola c'era l'attraente Miss Miss; non che lei sembrasse attratta da me, tanto che mi convinsi che sarebbe stata più incline a sfrattarmi dal corridoio piuttosto che ad accogliermi nella stanza da letto.

Misi in pratica la mia nuova condizione di turista mettendomi in fila per comprare una manciata di cozze e due uova da *Marcel's Casserole*.

Pensai che avrei dovuto sbalordirla, così che mi avrebbe guardato con occhi diversi da quelli con cui aveva guardato il randagio illuso e malridotto che aveva raccolto sulla spiaggia. Continuai comunque a pensare che doveva aver notato qualcosa di diverso in me dalla moltitudine di miserabili che erano giunti lì, per arrivare a invitarmi così spensieratamente ad entrare nella sua casa. Era stato forse il mio aspetto mite? Le mie origini straniere? I miei stivali di gomma color vinaccia con le suole nere? Una naturale signorilità?

L'uovo era così disgustosamente amaro da strapparmi una smorfia, ma continuai comunque a mangiarlo.

Un'anziana donna mi sfiorò col suo cappello nero chiodato, che per poco non mi cavò un occhio. Sembrava che avesse in testa un enorme riccio di mare. Camminava spedita, con fare irritato. La seguiva chiacchierando un uomo in giacca e cravatta, che le si rivolgeva chiamandola „madre".

Tra la folla, in piedi davanti alla Penrose Trading Company, scorsi una coppia di gentiluomini che catturarono la mia attenzione, apparentemente diversi da quell'accozzaglia di viaggiatori mordi e fuggi, e sgattaiolai dietro di loro.

Erano vestiti con abiti pesanti: spesse bluse, ampi cappotti e raffinati stivali di pelle. Portavano con sé un carrello pieno di attrezzi: pistole, gabbie, una discreta quantità di corda nuova di zecca, taniche d'acqua e altri stivali di pelle.

Non riuscivo a sentire cose dicessero, ma stavano discutendo di una mappa: non si trattava di una normale cartina stradale, con i luoghi d'interesse evidenziati, ma di un grande foglio disteso che avevano non poca difficoltà a tenere aperto a causa del vento, ricoperto da antiche linee, punti e simboli.

Intaccai il secondo uovo.

EPILOGO

Questa è la pianura in cui una volta Rocco ha trovato il corpo di un mostro. Mi perdo totalmente nella sua fluidità.

Moltitudini di bianchi fiori circolari si dissolvono nell'infinito anello di luce all'orizzonte; attorno solo il vento, che increspa i prati.

A tratti mi sembra di scorgere, al limite del visibile, qualche piccolo animale scappar via, ma non so dire se alcuna di queste visioni sia reale.

Finisco per fissare lo sguardo in basso, setacciando il terreno alla ricerca di un qualunque elemento di contrasto. Un piccolo sasso piatto ... i resti di una minuscola creatura, morta ormai da tempo ... forse ... strane linee sinusoidi nella polvere ... una qualche sostanza schiumosa sopra uno stelo ... un altro sasso ... una vecchia bottiglia di plastica! Capovolta e scossa, rilascia un liquido torbido che scompare nel terreno.

In molti si sono avventurati nella parte più remota di quest'isola dimenticata. Alcuni tornano per raccontarlo. Quelli che affermano di essere giunti alla ricerca di qualcosa d'ignoto, perché ogni cacciatore crede che, in quest'atmosfera rarefatta, viva una creatura chiamata Noumeno. L'esistenza di questa creatura non è mai stata provata, eppure si è radicata la convinzione che esista e viva qui, in questo territorio selvaggio, essendo ormai il resto dell'isola già stato tracciato sulle carte.

Alcuni giungono soli in modo da non spaventare la creatura, sperando piuttosto di ammaliarla – nessun avvistamento di questi solitari è stato accantonato, poiché l'altitudine conduce all'allucinazione i bramosi e alla falsificazione i ciarlatani. Altri giungono in coppia per avere un testimone, ma nessuno ha avuto successo. Quando si parla di Noumeno, in tre si è già troppi.

Sono poi comparse grandi imprese i cui rappresentanti, a centinaia, hanno soggiornato qui con cani, reti e trappole d'ogni sorta, cercando invano di circondare la creatura. Si tratta evidentemente di un essere infinitamente scaltro. La sua esistenza è sostenuta soltanto dalla fede o, come narra l'Arguzia Urbana: va al di là di ogni comprensione.

Esiste tuttavia un oceano di amnesia che le nuove generazioni devono attraversare per giungere sull'isola, e mentre trascinano le loro barche a riva e assaporano l'aria umida, ogni spedizione con un equipaggiamento nuovo, una scena popolata dai volti gioviali di giovani uomini e donne sulla spiaggia, pervasi di ottimismo mentre si dirigono verso l'oscurità.

Anch'io sono stato attirato qui dal profumo di questo enigmatico gatto, e ancora ho rimpianti. Mi accontenterei volentieri della sola illusione dei suoi escrementi, se soltanto potessi essere liberato dalla situazione in cui mi trovo adesso.

Sono disgustato dalla debolezza del mio carattere, dal dover ammettere che una solitudine malata mi ha pervaso più velocemente e più profondamente di quanto potessi immaginare. Mi struggo al pensiero di poter tornare alla situazione marginalmente molto meno solitaria del caffè agli avamposti di Onomatopy, dove per la prima volta si è affacciata l'idea di questa maldestra spedizione. Dove un cameriere scortese mi versò il caffè facendone cadere un bel po' nella salsa, prendendo poi a scherzare con il barman e a fare commenti osceni su femmine inaccessibili (alla sua rozzezza, alla mia timidezza) che passavano davanti alla vetrina. Dove due giganti con cappelli inverosimili si sedettero sorprendentemente vicino a uno specchio sulla parete, assorti in conversazione.

Un mendicante che vagava per il locale mi borbottò qualcosa in dialetto riguardo al latte per il suo bambino (assente) – facendomi intendere che voleva del denaro – e rimase a ciondolare per alcuni secondi dopo il mio rifiuto, facendomi inalare il suo fetore. Accidenti, pensai, perché i camerieri non intervengono e cacciano questo fannullone dal locale. Con mio disappunto, si sedette al bar,

dando del tu allo staff e bevve un caffè, che gli venne servito impeccabilmente; apparentemente di casa, scambiò saluti amichevoli con i giganti seduti nell'angolo.

Ma sono lontano da Onomatopy, e non conosco la strada verso casa; la morte sembra persino più vicina della città.

Ieri ho visto passare in lontananza quella lepre presuntuosa. Si è fermata per un momento guardando nella mia direzione, con uno sguardo che mi è parso di compassione. Ho sperato che potesse indicarmi la direzione verso casa, invece ha soltanto fatto brillare i suoi anelli verso di me, passando oltre. Con un riflesso ritardato, ho cercato invano di caricare il fucile con un paio di cartucce, ma la lepre era già lontana.

Un altro cacciatore una volta mi ha detto che tutto ciò che vali davvero fuori da qui equivale al contenuto del tuo zaino, a te stesso e al tuo fucile. Devi concentrarti per ricordarti chi sei; ecco perché ho iniziato a scrivere, per aiutarmi a ricordare. Non basta pensare: devi pensare "sto pensando!"

Ogni giorno – un evento delicato a queste latitudini – faccio un inventario per restare integro, o almeno per mantenere una distanza dalle cose:

Me stesso: Mi facio chiamare Only McFew (davvero!). Il mio migliore amico è una ragazza – la chiamo Miss Miss. Sono innamorato di lei, ma lei non lo sa, o fa finta di non vederlo. Sono un uomo.

Zaino: due matite. Un taccuino. Un barattolo. E un coltello, naturalmente, con cui poter spellare quella dannata lepre quando sarà diventata troppo sfacciata. Metà sacchetto di fette di banana essiccate. Un serpente con un braccio solo. Io metterò assieme all'altro che ho a casa, se mai vi farò ritorno. Li monterò su staffe di legno a elle e li userò come reggilibri. È un pensiero confortante. Un foratoio, proprietà adorata di Miss Miss che mi ha prestato diverso tempo fa (un elemento pesante da portarsi dietro e totalmente inutile nelle mie attuali circostanze.) Lo porto con me perché ho dimenticato di toglierlo dallo zaino prima di partire e non ho fatto caso al peso, per via della mia euforia all'inizio della spedizione.

I miei pensieri vagano verso una meditazione erotica su Miss Miss.

So di essere sulla vetta del mondo perché i fiori appaiono vividi contro un cielo plumbeo e riesco a sentire rumori senza causa apparente, piccole esplosioni melodiche nell'aria – un fenomeno che deve essere vissuto per poter essere creduto, come i pesci volanti, di cui ho sentito parlare dai marinai (e a cui non credo).

Mi sento come se stessi camminando di fianco al tempo, col passato sulla sinistra e il futuro alla mia destra. Non posso continuare così. Devo fare una scelta, ma so che non lo farò, per paura che sia quella sbagliata. Quindi continuo, un piede davanti all'altro, sperando che un segno giunga a indicarmi la strada.

E al contempo, cosa peggiore di tutte, ho iniziato a dubitare. Dubito seriamente del Noumeno, e mi chiedo se non ho messo a rischio la mia vita, sacrificato le mie ossa alla polvere anonima della vallata in nome di una chimera (penso che la lepre si avvicinerà guardinga al mio cadavere dopo essersi assicurata che sia davvero morto senza poter risorgere, e quando la carne delle mie dita si sarà putrefatta, si prenderà il mio anello con granato per aggiungerlo alla sua collezione.)

Dubito dell'affetto di Miss Miss, o che il suo sé fatalista possa vedere la mia fine come qualcosa di diverso dal semplice fluire degli eventi.

Anche altre cose hanno iniziato a disturbarmi: alcune volte i fiori non si allineano bene sugli steli. Perché non ho mai visto la vetta di una montagna? Nonostante i miei sforzi pazienti nello studio della lingua If'enish, non ho appreso che poche parole, lasciandomi col sospetto che questo dialetto non sia altro che un gergo astruso, improvvisato per la gioia dei turisti.

Infine, ho iniziato a chiedermi se, al di là dei negozi, dei bar e delle luci di Onomatopy, oltre il piano degli Dei, dove le macchine in disuso e i rifiuti vengono sparsi, al di sotto delle montagne, dei fiori, della polvere e delle ossa dei cacciatori, ci sia davvero un'isola.

Questo testo è stato originariamente commissionato nel 2009 per la quarta uscita di To Hell with Journals pubblicato da Charles Arsène-Henry e Hans Ulrich Obrist.

ADDENDA

Questo libro è stato realizzato in occasione della mostra di Charles Avery dal titolo *Onomatopoeia: part 1* allestita presso Le Plateau / Frac Île-de-France, Parigi; the Kunstverein Hannover; ed EX3, Firenze.

Sin dal 2005 Charles Avery ha lavorato su un corpus formalmente epico dal quale emerge, attraverso disegni, progetti, installazioni e testi, un'Isola immaginaria.
L'Isola – che non ha altro nome – è collocata al centro di un arcipelago a spirale formato da innumerevoli isole più piccole, sommerse da un oceano nero. La nostra conoscenza di questa *terra incognita* ci giunge attraverso la testimonianza di un ragazzo del quale non sapremo mai il nome; approdato su una costa remota dell'Isola, dopo aver creduto di esserne lo scopritore viene ben presto disilluso da una ragazza incontrata sulla spiaggia e forzato a rivedere radicalmente la propria *raison d'être*.

The Islanders può essere interpretato in molti modi diversi: meditazione sui temi centrali della filosofia, critica di tutti i grandi dualismi, quali conscio e subconscio, realtà e immaginazione, singolarità e pluralità o metafora della spartizione e del dominio puramente coloniali del mondo delle idee.

Nel 2008 la Parasol unit di Londra ha ospitato la prima grande mostra sul progetto, semplicemente intitolata "The Islanders: an introduction", successivamente allestita alla Gallery of Modern Art di Edinburgo ed al Museum Boijmans van Beuningen di Rotterdam. La mostra e il relativo libretto intendevano descrivere le caratteristiche fondamentali dell'Isola, nonché offrire un panorama dell'intero progetto come "work in progress", definendo al contempo le aspirazioni e la portata dell'impresa futura. Da quel momento, il progetto si è incentrato sull'esplorazione dettagliata dell'unica città presente sull'Isola, quella di Onomatopoeia, che, da vecchio avamposto coloniale, si è trasformata in boomtown e in un fiorente centro commerciale, per poi degenerare in luogo malfamato e di nuovo rinascere come destinazione turistica.

Gli eventi allestiti presso Le Plateau / Frac Île-de-France, Parigi; the Kunstverein Hannover ed EX3, Firenze costituiscono le prime grandi mostre di questa importante fase del progetto, oltre ad essere le prime personali a carattere istituzionale dell'opera dell'artista rispettivamente in Francia, Germania e Italia.

Questo libro è dedicato ad un unico, grande disegno (2,4 m di altezza per più di 5 m di lunghezza) del porto di Onomatopoeia che, punto di arrivo e di partenza da e verso questo regno immaginario, costituisce un punto focale della città, nonché dell'Isola, racchiudendo perfettamente in sé l'intero progetto.

I direttori desiderano ringraziare Charles Avery per il suo straordinario impegno nella realizzazione delle mostre e nella pubblicazione, Marc Kappeler per il design grafico del catalogo e le gallerie doggerfisher, Edinburgo, Pilar Corrias, Londra e Sonia Rosso, Torino per il loro sostegno organizzativo e finanziario.

Per il loro appoggio al progetto nelle singole località di mostra, Le Plateau / Frac Île-de-France, Parigi, desidera ringraziare le Conseil régional d'Île-de-France, le Ministère de la culture et de la communication und la Ville de Paris, il Kunstverein di Hannover ringrazia il Ministero della scienza e della cultura dello Stato della Bassa Sassonia, il NORD / LB, e lo Stiftung Horizonte, nonché EX3 che ringrazia il Comune di Firenze e il Progetto toscanaincontemporanea della Regione Toscana

Xavier Franceschi
Direttore, Le Plateau / Frac Île-de-France, Parigi

René Zechlin
Direttore, Kunstverein Hannover

Sergio Tossi
Direttore, EX3, Firenze

This book has been published on the occasion of the exhibitions *Onomatopoeia, part 1* by Charles Avery in:

Le Plateau / Frac Île-de-France, Paris, France
May 26 – August 8, 2010
Curator: Xavier Franceschi

Kunstverein Hannover, Germany
August 28 – November 7, 2010
Curator: René Zechlin

Ex3 Centro per l'arte contemporanea, Firenze, Italy
November 17, 2010 – January 9th, 2011
Curators: Lorenzo Giusti, Arabella Natalini

Image:
Charles Avery
Untitled
(View of the Port at Onomatopoeia),
2009–2010
Pencil and ink on paper, 240 x 510 cm
Courtesy Galerie Pilar Corrias, London

Edited by: Le Plateau / Frac Ile-de-France, Paris, Kunstverein Hannover, Germany, EX3, Firenze, Italy
Texts: Charles Avery
Publication's coordinator: Maëlle Dault
Design: Moiré, Marc Kappeler, Markus Reichenbach & Dominik Huber, Zurich
Translation from English to French: Maxime Boidy
Translation from English to German: Karl Hoffmann
Translation from English to Italian: Ernest Vaudry
Typeface: Platten
Paper: Munken Lynx 150g
Printing: Druckerei Odermatt, Dallenwil
Binding: Buchbinderei Schumacher, Schmitten

First published by Koenig Books, London

Koenig Books Ltd
At the Serpentine Gallery
Kensington Gardens
London W2 3XA
www.koenigbooks.co.uk

Printed in Switzerland

Charles Avery is represented by doggerfisher, Edinburgh, Pilar Corrias Gallery, London and Galleria Sonia Rosso, Torino

In addition to all the individuals mentioned above Charles Avery would like to thank Michael Lewis, Martin Johnson, Dorothea Avery, Pilar Corrias, Sonia Rosso, and Susanna Beaumont, without whose support this project would not have been possible.

Distribution:

Verlag der Buchhandlung
Walther König, Köln
Ehrenstr. 4, 50672 Köln
Tel. +49 (0) 221 / 20 59 6 53
Fax +49 (0) 221 / 20 59 6 60
verlag@buchhandlung-walther-koenig.de

Switzerland
Buch 2000
c/o AVA Verlagsauslieferungen AG
Centralweg 16
CH-8910 Affoltern a.A.
Tel. +41 (44) 762 42 00
Fax +41 (44) 762 42 10
a.koll@ava.ch

UK & Eire
Cornerhouse Publications
70 Oxford Street
GB-Manchester M1 5NH
Fon +44 (0) 161 200 15 03
Fax +44 (0) 161 200 15 04
publications@cornerhouse.org

Outside Europe
D.A.P. / Distributed Art Publishers, Inc.
155 6th Avenue, 2nd Floor
USA-New York, NY 10013
Fon +1 212 627 1999
Fax +1 212 627 9484
www.artbook.com

ISBN 978-3-86560-840-6

Frac Île-de-France
Le Plateau

President: François Barré
Director: Xavier Franceschi
General Secretary: Sumiko Oe-Gottini
Management assistant:
Anne-Claire Duprat
Exhibition and Publishing assistant:
Maëlle Dault
Communication: Isabelle Fabre
Press: Magda Kachouche
Coordinator of the Permanent
Collection: Veerle Dobbeleir
Publics service: Gilles Baume,
Marie Baloup
Extra teacher (Académie de Créteil):
Judicaël Lavrador
Receptionist: Magali Arbogast
Technicians: Frédéric Daugu,
Julien Pettex-Muffat

Frac Île-de-France / Le Plateau
33 rue des alouettes
F-75019 Paris – France
Tél +33 (0) 1 53 19 88 10
Fax +33 (0) 1 53 19 88 19
info@fracidf-leplateau.com
www.fracidf-leplateau.com

The Frac Île-de-France is an initiative of the Conseil régional d'Île-de-France. The Frac Île-de-France is supported by the Ministry of Culture and Communication – Direction régionale des affaires culturelles, in its activities involving Le Plateau, by the Ville de Paris. The Frac Île-de-France is a member of the following networks: tram, platform, the Frac group, DCA and Grand Belleville.

îledeFrance

Culture Communication

MAIRIE DE PARIS

<< PLATFORM >>

tram

kunst verein hannover

Director: René Zechlin
Curator: Ute Stuffer
Assistance and Coordination:
Angela Lautenbach
Art Handling and accountancy:
Marina Neufang
Technical department: Rolf Risse
Public relations: Katharina Klara Jung
Education: Andrea Gogl (freelance)
Technical crew: Mathieu Cortin,
Isabel Henn, Christian Nolting,
Andreas Schüßler, Gerhard Wiegmann
Interns: Gesa Antonia Kaselow,
Aileen Kagemann

Board: Ellen Lorenz, Jörg Maaß,
Dr. Jürgen Peters, Gerlinde Harig
Advisory council: Jens Adolf,
Peter Allmann, Degenhard Andrulat,
Stefan Becker, Philipp Benatzky,
Heidi Dunkel, Peter Gauditz,
Christoph Girardet, Anna Grunemann,
Robert Kroth, Andrea von Lüdinghausen,
Susanne Maaß, Christiane Oppermann,
Gabriele Sand, Jörg Stichnoth

Kunstverein Hannover
Sophienstraße 2
30159 hannover – Germany
Tel +49 (0) 511 16 99 278-0
Fax +49 (0) 511 16 99 278-278
mail@kunstverein-hannover.de
www.kunstverein-hannover.de

The exhibition at the Kunstverein Hannover has been supported generously by Land Niedersachsen, Stiftung Horizonte, NordLB.

Niedersächsisches Ministerium für Wissenschaft und Kultur

Stiftung Horizonte
Kunst & Kultur im Tschechischen Pavillon

NORD/LB

The Kunstverein Hannover is sponsored by the Culture Office of the Landeshauptstadt Hannover

Landeshauptstadt Hannover Kulturbüro

EX3

Director: Sergio Tossi
Curators: Lorenzo Giusti and
Arabella Natalini
Assistance and Coordination:
Leonardo Bressan
Exhibition rooms coordinator:
Massimo Bocconi
Press: Davis & Franceschini
Communication: Neri Torrigiani
Administration: Enrico Baluardi
President: Andrea Tanini
Vice President: Andrea Mannari
Board: Giorgio Cerrai, Massimo Dei,
Michele Legnaioli, Lucia Montigiani,
Claudio Nardi.

EX3
Viale Giannotti 81/83/85
50126 Firenze – Italy
Tel: +39 055 628 7091
info@ex3.it
www.ex3.it

EX3 is supported by Comune di Firenze – Assessorato alla Cultura e Contemporaneità, Assessorato allo Sviluppo Economico, Quartiere 3 and by Regione Toscana.

COMUNE DI FIRENZE

toscanaincontemporanea 2010